ONE SWEET YEAR OF Cupcakes

DELICIOUS FLAVORS FOR EVERY SEASON

ONE SWEET YEAR OF

Cupcakes

DELICIOUS FLAVORS FOR EVERY SEASON

FROM THE WINNER OF *CUPCAKE WARS* ON FOOD NETWORK

JANELL BROWN

FRONT TABLE BOOKS • AN IMPRINT OF CEDAR FORT, INC. • SPRINGVILLE, UTAH

ISBN: 978-1-4621-1451-1

PUBLISHED BY FRONT TABLE BOOKS, AN IMPRINT OF CEDAR FORT, INC.
2373 W. 700 S., SPRINGVILLE, UT, 84663
DISTRIBUTED BY CEDAR FORT, INC., WWW.CEDARFORT.COM

LIBRARY OF CONGRESS CATALOGING-IN-PUBLICATION DATA
    BROWN, JANELL, 1979-
    ONE SWEET YEAR OF CUPCAKES / JANELL BROWN.
       PAGES CM
    INCLUDES INDEX.
    ISBN 978-1-4621-1451-1 (ACID-FREE PAPER)
    1. CUPCAKES. 2. SEASONAL COOKING. I. TITLE.
    TX771.B8768 2014
    641.8'653--DC23
                            2014019510

COVER AND PAGE DESIGN BY BEKAH CLAUSSEN
COVER DESIGN © 2014 BY LYLE MORTIMER
EDITED BY HANNAH BALLARD AND RACHEL MUNK

PRINTED IN CHINA

10 9 8 7 6 5 4 3 2 1

PRAISE FOR *ONE SWEET YEAR OF CUPCAKES*

"*One Sweet Year of Cupcakes* is a delicious compilation of cupcake recipes for every season, created by award-winning cake decorator, Janelle Brown. If you haven't been to one of Janelle's One Sweet Slice stores, you can now bring a bit of heaven into your home. This cookbook not only includes mouthwatering recipes, but defines the important ingredients to have on hand, as well a summary of baking basics and step-by-step instructions for decorating. *One Sweet Year of Cupcakes* is the perfect addition to any kitchen!"

—HEATHER B. MOORE, USA TODAY BESTSELLING AUTHOR

"I love to cook, but I have never been much of a baker…until now! Janell explains the science of the perfect cupcake, and simplifies things so that even *I* can make her beautifully delicious treats. I love that this new book features the fresh tastes of each season, and I can't wait to try them and succeed!"

—MARY NICKLES, KUTV 2 NEWS ANCHOR/BEGINNER BAKER

"Janell is my go-to for exceptional desserts, cupcakes, custom cakes, and so much more. From a variety of mouthwatering flavors, choices, custom creations, and friendly customer service, I feel confident referring my clients to Janell. She delivers the highest of quality, with impeccable attention to detail in every product, no matter how custom or unique. My clients expect the very best, and when it comes to recommending the perfect cake or dessert for their important event, Janell is a guaranteed win all around."

—MICHELLE COUSINS, OWNER OF MICHELLE LEO EVENTS

"Janell has completely knocked it out of the park with *One Sweet Year of Cupcakes*. The Cupcake Wars Winner and owner of the award-winning One Sweet Slice Bakery will have you feeling like a cupcake connoisseur with her tips and tricks for making the perfect cupcake. The step-by-step instructions for each recipe are fool-proof, so ANYONE will be able to make these drool-worthy desserts. *One Sweet Year of Cupcakes* has a recipe for any event, no matter the time of year, that will leave your friends and family amazed and asking for more."

—STEPHANIE LOAIZA – COOKBOOK AUTHOR, CO-OWNER, AND SISTER NUMBER FOUR OF SIX SISTERS' STUFF.

"Janell has received national fame, but her Utah fans have known her cupcakes for a long time! As an excellent teacher, Janell's book is a great companion for the novice and experienced baker; chock full of deliciousness! I can't wait to try them all!"

—MARY CRAFTS-HOMER, CEO/PRESIDENT CULINARY CRAFTS

"There are few people who can take their unique artistic vision and translate it into a delicious, fun masterpiece. Janell is one of those people. Simply put, some people make gingerbread houses; Janell makes gingerbread stadiums."

—MATT BROWN, EXECUTIVE CHEF – LEVY RESTAURANTS

"Besides being addicted to Janell's award-winning cupcakes, she has inspired me to follow my dreams and has been a great source of inspiration and knowledge as we launch our new manufacturing facility. Her cupcakes are unique, sweet, and satisfying. I often step into her shop and get my favorite, the Grasshopper cupcake. You better believe I will be using her new book, *One Sweet Year Of Cupcakes,* for all SWEET events in our home. Much love to Janell, and wishing you continued success."

—PRISCILLA BRIGGS, CEO AND CURATOR – DESIGNER LOLLIPOP

CONTENTS

Spring

Summer

Icings

Fillings and Toppings

INTRODUCTION

I love to eat! This is the primary reason I enjoy baking. There is nothing more satisfying than taking raw ingredients like sugar, flour, eggs, milk, and so on, mixing them together in one form or another, and creating something that looks, smells, and tastes amazing. The world of baking provides a canvas for creativity. The possibilities of flavor combinations, textures, and presentation ideas are endless.

When I was asked to write a second cupcake book, I sat down and thought about where I should begin. I needed some inspiration. Like most people, I always get better ideas when I'm eating something, so I started to peel and slice a peach from the small peach tree in our backyard. Even though this tree is small, it has somehow managed to produce enough fruit every season for me to can twenty-six quarts of peaches! As I poured a little cream on top of the peach slices and sprinkled a touch of nutmeg across the top, I was reminded of how many summers I had spent helping my mother and grandmother pick and can peaches, apricots, apples, pears, currants, raspberries, and rhubarb. Fruit, like most things, always tastes best when eaten in season. That's when the idea came: Why not put together a cookbook that uses ingredients, flavors, and memories for each season?

While I don't have a mother and grandmothers who love to bake and have passed down family recipes, I do have a mother and grandmothers who understand and appreciate the importance of good, simple, fresh food. I grew up drinking fresh cow's milk and cream, not because it was a new hip thing to do, but because it was what we had. We planted a garden and canned the produce, not because of a pin on Pinterest, but because it was wise to do so and wasteful not to. Eating the best food you have available, in the season it is available, will result in some of the most delicious dishes of all time—in this case, wonderfully seasonal cupcakes! I hope you enjoy some of my favorite seasonal flavors and the memories that go with them. Tradition stems from small moments in life that are remembered and repeated year after year. My hope is that some of these recipes will become a part of those traditions and memories for you and your family!

ABOUT ME

I did not grow up dreaming to one day own a bakery. My first memories are not of my mother baking in the kitchen. Though I did have an appreciation for delicious baked goods when I was a child—what child doesn't?—and my favorite dessert was a warm gooey brownie with a cold glass of milk, my discovery of baking was unplanned and came later in life.

At the age of ten, I picked up a few bottles of acrylic paint from my mother's stash and started to repaint my bedroom. My favorite part of my science fair projects was decorating the board, and I enjoyed trying to make our Sunday boxed mix cakes look like something from a Betty Crocker magazine. I love being creative, working with what I have, and making things that taste amazing and look beautiful. Combining the creativity of making something beautiful and making something delicious was a great challenge.

At age twenty-five I had just received my bachelor's degree in interpersonal communications, and was expecting the birth of our first son. One month later, I started to take cake decorating classes at a local craft store, to develop a new hobby and to give myself a night out each week. I quickly fell in love with the creative outlet cake decorating provided, and the idea of using sugar as an art medium was incredible—art you can eat! After completing the three-month course, I began assisting my instructor and taught basic cake decorating classes for two years. Making cakes became my favorite pastime, and I filled my weekends with orders for family and friends. During this time I was expecting our third baby. After her birth, I decided to quit teaching and started a small cake-decorating business at home.

The state of Utah allows you to run a licensed kitchen from your home. After completing tedious paperwork, having my home inspected, and explaining to my children that after eight o'clock the kitchen was closed, I set up shop. I began by posting an ad in the local classified section of Salt Lake City's online newspaper. With a few unprofessional pictures and a discounted price of one hundred dollars for a three-tiered wedding cake, I hesitantly offered my services as a cake decorator. By the end of the first month, I had five wedding cakes booked, and I had even charged one bride the staggering price of two hundred dollars! I had three small children under the age of three, so all of my baking and decorating had to be done at night after they had gone to bed. I spent many late nights mixing, baking, icing, and decorating. I became a night owl and looked forward to the long hours of listening to my old high school music and talking with my husband Trent while I worked. It was during one of these conversations that the name "One Sweet Slice" evolved. The name was selected because: first, the website address was available, and second, I felt it represented what I was trying to do. I was creating cakes that would help celebrate some of the sweetest moments in life! Events that were a slice out of the ordinary. Trent set up a small website, and he began to market our little business online. Word of mouth began to spread and requests started to pour in.

For six years I balanced my love of cake decorating, love for my family, and everything that comes with a fast paced, young, always chaotic, and slightly messy household. Trent supported me in every way possible. Often I would find him letting me sleep in, fixing dinner, playing with neglected children, kneading fondant, and delivering cakes. When I became overly tired or discouraged, instead of telling me to quit, he would offer suggestions or look for ways he could help. He was the only one who consistently saw how much work went on behind the scenes, and understood and supported my crazy desire to keep baking and cake decorating a part of my life.

In December 2010, three days after Christmas, opportunity knocked. My husband had been laid off from work, I was six weeks away from delivering our fourth child and was looking forward to having a few months to relax and focus on my new baby. Little did I know the next few months would be full of stress, major decisions, sleepless nights, and life-changing events! Always an entrepreneur at heart, Trent expressed the desire to start his own business, and after looking at our options, we decided to join forces. We made the decision to open our shop while I was in the hospital with our new baby! Four months and a ridiculous amount of work later, we opened the doors of our One Sweet Slice Custom Cake and Cupcake shop.

During our first year we won multiple awards, were featured in many magazines, and appeared on a few different television shows in Utah. In September 2012, we competed on the Food Network's *Cupcake Wars*. After a lot of hard work, we beat out the competition and won! Being asked to compete on the Food Network was a chance of a lifetime. My good friend and pastry extraordinaire Kristen Cold competed with me on the Star Wars Challenge. It was incredible to see the amount of work and talent the producers and competitors put into each episode. The thrill of winning a televised national competition and winning ten thousand dollars is something I'll never forget. Winning the *Cupcake Wars* has opened countless doors of opportunity and has changed our lives. We now have a second location in Utah and continue to look for ways to share our passion for cake with everyone.

My hope in writing both of my books is to share what I love and what I have learned about the art of baking a beautiful and delicious cupcake—or at least one sweet slice.

INGREDIENTS

One purpose in writing this book was to create a collection of recipes that are delicious, unique, easy to follow, and that can be made with accessible and recognizable ingredients.

There is nothing more frustrating than getting halfway through a recipe and discovering that you don't have one of the ingredients, or even worse—that you've never heard of it, and have no idea where to buy it! This always seems to happen on a Sunday night—for some reason cupcakes always taste better on a Sunday night—and the last thing I want you to do is make a trip to the grocery store, or send one of your kids to a neighbor's house asking for something that neither of you can pronounce (note: you can always blame the mispronunciation on your kids if needed).

These recipes are created with ingredients you can find at any local grocery store, and at least one out of five neighbors will have what you need if you don't already have it in your pantry. I grew up in a very small town with one grocery store, and the closest Walmart was an hour away. Our "natural" food store was my mother's garden, or my grandmother's five-year supply of canned fruit, fresh jams and preserves, hand-ground wheat, homemade yogurt, or warm cream scraped from the top of a pitcher of milk. Everything grown was used for cooking, baking, or a health remedy of some sort. The unspoken motto was, "Use what you have." I believe it is important to use the best ingredients that you have. The better your ingredients are, the better your end product will be. I also believe in practicality. It is not necessary to have organic farm eggs, or cocoa that costs a ridiculous amount of money and can only be found in a store you don't regularly shop at, to create an incredible tasting cupcake. If you feel strongly about all natural, organic, and shopping local, then purchase your ingredients from the shops you frequent. If you prefer the convenience and pricing of a box store, then purchase your ingredients there. Use the best you can!

A few key ingredients to have on hand before you begin baking:

Butter: Unsalted butter is a must when baking. If at all possible, use only real butter and not margarine. Butter adds flavor and texture to your baking. The temperature of the butter is also very important in baking. Always use room temperature butter, never cold. This allows the maximum amount of air to be beaten into your batter. Beating the butter first, before adding the other ingredients, will create air bubbles that the baking powder will enlarge during baking. Butter is essential for creating delicious icing, so do not substitute it.

Milk: The extra fat in whole milk adds another layer of flavor to your cupcakes, and acts as a tenderizer and moisturizer. Your cake will have a more delicate crumb, and will not be dry. In these recipes, the milk does not need to be at room temperature. Buttermilk is the liquid left after the butter was churned, and creates a light tang in the taste of vanilla based cakes. It is an acidic ingredient, like yogurt or sour cream, and helps tenderize the gluten in the batter and the cake to rise.

Eggs: Always use large eggs when baking. Eggs act as a leavening agent and add color, texture, flavor, and richness to the batter. They help to bind the other ingredients together. The air from beaten eggs acts as a leavening agent when it expands in the oven and causes the cake to rise. Eggs are also used to thicken custards, curds, and creams. The egg whites are used to make meringues. For these recipes, the eggs do not need to be at room temperature.

Sour cream: Sour cream is made from cultured cream. It acts as an emulsifier by holding the cake together, and will give your cake a velvety texture. It has a very high fat content and adds a rich flavor.

Vegetable oil: Canola oil is the ideal choice to use when baking. It is light, flavorless, and inexpensive. The oil acts as a bonding agent and is essential in adding moisture to the cake.

Baking powder: Baking powder is a leavening agent that will cause batters to rise when baked. After the ingredients are creamed together, the leavener enlarges the air bubbles in the batter while the cupcakes are in the oven. Baking powder contains baking soda, cream of tartar, and cornstarch.

Salt: Salt is a flavor enhancer, and even though a small amount is used, it is crucial to baking! There are three different types of salt that can be used: iodized salt or table salt, kosher salt, and sea salt. If it has a fine grain, all three types can be used for baking.

Flour: Flour can be ground from a variety of nuts and seeds. These recipes call for wheat flour. Even among wheat flour there are many different types of flour, and the type you use will ultimately affect the finished product. Because flour contains protein, it will produce gluten when it comes into contact with water and heat. The gluten gives elasticity and strength to baked goods. All-purpose flour is ideal for cupcakes and is used in each of these recipes.

Sugar: Many types of sugars are available, but three are used in these recipes: granulated, brown, and powdered. Sugar is produced from sugar cane or beets, and has been refined to small white granules. Brown sugar is refined white sugar with some of the molasses left, giving it a brown color. Powdered or confectioners sugar is sugar that has been ground to a powder and has cornstarch added to reduce clumping and aid in thickening.

Sugar does more than just sweeten cupcake batter. When sugar and butter are creamed together, the sugar granules rub against the fat in the butter and produce air bubbles. When the leavener is added, the gases enlarge the bubbles, causing the batter to rise when the cupcakes are placed in the oven. Sugar also has the ability to hold moisture, resulting in a tender cake crumb and a long shelf life. It is the sugar and butter together in the batter that causes cupcakes to brown during baking.

Chocolate: There are two types of unsweetened cocoa powder: Dutch processed or unsweetened. Dutch-processed is treated with an alkali to neutralize its acids. It has a reddish-brown color and a light flavor, and is easy to dissolve. Unsweetened cocoa is very bitter and gives a deep, intense chocolate flavor.

Vanilla: This extract is used in every cupcake recipe and is extremely important. Pure vanilla extract, not vanilla flavoring should be used. The extract comes from vanilla beans harvested in Central America, and provides a rich and delicious flavor to each recipe. Infusing crushed vanilla beans into a sweet syrup creates vanilla bean paste. Using the paste will leave small flecks of vanilla bean in the batter.

SEASONAL INGREDIENTS

Watermelon: The watermelon is a vegetable. It is part of the cucumber, squash, and pumpkin family. To find a ripe melon, look for one that is free of dents and bruises, and has a yellow or light bottom. If the melon has stripes all around it, it is not ready yet. Often people will tap on a watermelon to see if it's ripe. If the melon sounds hollow it is ripe; if it doesn't sound hollow, it's unripe. The last thing to look for is the weight of the melon. Watermelons are made primarily of water, so an ideal melon should feel heavy for its size.

Oranges: Originating in Southeast Asia, oranges were cultivated in China, some think as far back as 2500 BC. The Spaniards introduced the oranges to the American continent in the mid-1500s.[1] So how do you pick a good orange? The heavier the orange, the juicier it will be. Next, check the scent. Make sure it smells fresh, not musty or moldy. Finally look at the color. The orange color should be uniform with no spots or shriveling.

Tangerines: This delicious fruit is believed to have originated in China, and has been cultivated in China and Japan for over 3,000 years! After arriving in Europe in Tangier, Morocco for the first time, they adopted the name tangerines.[2] They are a great source for vitamin C. There are a few primary differences between oranges and tangerines. The tangerine is smaller in size, less acidic, and the peel is much easier to remove.[3] As an added bonus, the word *tangerine* is much more fun to say.

Pumpkins: Pumpkins are used for more than just carving. They were once moved to remove freckles and cure snake bites![4] We like it best in cupcakes, of course. If you choose to make your own pumpkin purée, select a small sugar pumpkin, about the size of a volleyball.[5] Leave the large pumpkins for jack-o-lanterns.

Lemons: Who would have guessed that the lemon comes from an evergreen tree! The tree blooms a white flower and produces fruit all year round. Christopher Columbus brought lemon seeds with him when he sailed for the new world back in 1492.[6] Lemons have a distinct flavor that dessert lovers can't get enough of. It can be paired with such a wide variety of fruits that the flavor possibilities are endless.

Limes: Some believe that the lime originated in Persia. Today the most commonly used limes come from Mexico. The fruit is picked green when they are between one and two inches in diameter. When picked small, they have a sharper, more acidic flavor.[7] There is a difference between a "Persian" lime and a Key lime. Key limes are much smaller, have a thinner skin, and are green and yellow in appearance. They are very juicy and have a strong aroma and a higher acidic level regular limes.[8] This makes them ideal for baking!

Raspberries: Although we use primarily red raspberries in our cupcake baking, they can be red, purple, gold, or black in color. In the United States about 90 percent of the raspberries we use come from Washington, Oregon, and California. Raspberries need to be picked when they are fully ripened because once picked, they won't ripen any further.[9]

Pineapple: Believe it or not, it takes almost three years for one pineapple to reach it's full maturation! And although I beg to differ, once harvested they don't continue to ripen.[10] So pick your pineapple wisely. Here's how: First smell the pineapple, it should smell sweet and ripe, but it should not smell so ripe that is seems fermented. Second, look at the pineapple, it should be golden brown in color, with no withering leaves, and no signs of mold. Try to buy pineapples that are grown closest to where you live. And finally, feel the pineapple. It should feel firm but give slightly when squeezed, and if it feels heavy, it will be nice and juicy inside.[11]

Pecans: The United States produces 80–95 percent of the world's pecans from more than 10,000 trees![12] Before a shelled pecan is ready to be sold, it needs to be cleaned, sized, sterilized, cracked, and shelled.[13] That sounds like a lot of work for such a little nut. But it's worth the work! Pecans have a delicious buttery flavor that works perfectly with chocolate or vanilla flavors, and they taste wonderful in or on top of cupcakes.

Macadamia Nuts: Most people think of Hawaii when this nut is mentioned, but it originated in Australia and were eaten and traded by the Aborigine tribes long before it made its way to the islands. They are high in fat and low in protein, making them tasty, but not very healthy. Macadamia nuts are also toxic to dogs, so no sharing these puppies![14]

Cinnamon: Smelling the scent of cinnamon can boost brain activity.[15] What better excuse could you have to make cupcakes with cinnamon in them! It comes from the inner bark of cinnamon trees and is ground into a fine powder creating a spice. It is one of the oldest spices known and was used in ancient Egypt as a beverage flavoring, and medicine, and aided in the embalming process. It was considered more precious than gold.[16] Get ready to indulge!

Rhubarb: Long before baking, rhubarb was used in China for medicinal purposes. It is technically a vegetable, not a fruit, but who's keeping score? It grows in stalks like celery and is very tart and sour in taste.[17] In baking, rhubarb tastes best when paired with a sweet fruit like strawberries.

Honey: Honey is the only food source humans consume that is produced by an insect. Sounds gross, until you taste it. Honey is a Hebrew word meaning "to enchant." It has been used as a culinary sweetener and a healing ingredient. Its use dates back for 150 million years and was written about in hieroglyphics. Honey soaks up moisture rapidly and is an excellent ingredient for helping cakes and cookies last longer.[18] When measuring with honey, be sure to coat the spoon or cup with a small amount of cooking spray so the honey will not stick. Honey makes any dessert taste just a little more divine.

Blackberries: Blackberries are healthy! The dark blue color of their skin lets us know they contain one of the highest level of antioxidants of all fruits. Antioxidants can lower the risk of cancer, and blackberry leaves can be used to treat inflamed gums and sore throats, so eat up![19]

Notes:

1. Morton, Julia F. "Fruits of Warm Climates." Pittman and Davis (1987): 134-142. Accessed June 6 2014. http://www.hort.purdue.edu/newcrop/morton/orange.html.

2. "12 Facts About Tangerines." *Eat This!* (2009). Accessed June 6, 2014. http://www.healthdiaries.com/eatthis/12-facts-about-tangerines.html.

3. "Difference Between Orange and Tangerine" *Difference Between.* Accessed June 6, 2014. http://www.differencebetween.net/object/difference-between-orange-and-tangerine/.

4. "Fun and Interesting Autumn Facts." *Live Psychics Network* (2013). Accessed June 6, 2014. http://blog.livepsychicsnetwork.com/uncategorized/fun-and-interesting-autumn-facts/.

5. "Baking with Pumpkin: Making Your Own Fresh Pumpkin Purée is Easy." *King Arthur Flour* (2011). Accessed June 6, 2014. http://www.kingarthurflour.com/blog/2011/10/24/baking-with-pumpkin-making-your-own-fresh-pumpkin-purée-is-easy/.

6. "Lemon Facts for Kids" *Science Kids.* Accessed June 6, 2014. http://www.sciencekids.co.nz/sciencefacts/food/lemons.html.

7. Barth, Brian. "Interesting Facts About Limes." *Home Guides.* Accessed June 6, 2014. http://homeguides.sfgate.com/interesting-limes-90216.html.

8. "Yes Virginia, There is a Key Lime." Accessed June 6, 2014. http://www.keylime.com/diff.html.

9. Jones, Joanne. "Interesting Facts About Raspberries." Accessed June 6, 2014. http://EzineArticles.com/2347577.

10. "17 Mind-Boggling Facts About Pineapples." *Huffington Post* (2014). Accessed June 6, 2014. http://www.huffingtonpost.com/2014/02/04/facts-about-pineapples_n_4726366.html.

11. "How to Tell if a Pineapple Is Ripe." *wikiHow.* Accessed June 6, 2014. http://www.wikihow.com/Tell-if-a-Pineapple-Is-Ripe.

12. "How Nutty! Fun Facts About Pecans." *I Love Pecans.* Accessed June 6, 2014. http://www.ilove-pecans.org/pecans-101/fun-facts-about-pecans/.

13. "Pecan." *Wikipedia.* Accessed June 6, 2014. http://en.wikipedia.org/wiki/Pecan.

14. "Macadamia." *Wikipedia.* Accessed June 6, 2014. http://en.wikipedia.org/wiki/Macadamia#History.

15. Rutherford-Fortunati, Alisa. "6 Surprising Facts About Cinnamon. Accessed June 6, 2014. http://www.care2.com/greenliving/6-suprising-facts-about-cinnamon.html#ixzz2yve2ABeI.

16. Lopez-McHugh, Nancy. "10 Cinnamon Facts You Should Know." *Honest Cooking* (2012). http://honestcooking.com/10-cinnamon-facts-you-should-know/.

17. Angelo White, Dana. "5 Things You Didn't Know About Rhubarb." *Food Network (2011).* Accessed June 6, 2014. http://blog.foodnetwork.com/healthyeats/2011/06/06/5-rhubarb-facts-and-recipes/?oc=linkback.

18. Piper, Lori. "Ten Interesting Facts About Honey." *Yahoo Voices.* Accessed June 6, 2014. http://voices.yahoo.com/ten-interesting-facts-honey-511381.html.

19. Simms, Dileen. "Blackberry Facts" Ten Things You May Not Know About the Fruit." *Huffington Post* (2013). Accessed June 6, 2014. http://www.huffingtonpost.ca/2013/01/31/blackberry-facts_n_2581622.html.

BAKING BASICS

Let's start at the very beginning. It is a very good place to start, after all. The basics of baking involve good ingredients, proper equipment, and a great recipe. Buy the best ingredients available to you and have all of the equipment you need before you begin. The equipment you use in baking is an investment—do it right.

Follow the steps in the order found in each recipe. There is science and reason to the purpose and order of each step.

Do not overmix your batter. A few minutes is all that is needed; any more will result in a hard, chewy, un-delicious cupcake.

Use fresh fruit whenever possible.

Use an oven thermometer and don't forget to set the timer. It is always better to underbake and let the cupcakes bake a little longer with your watchful eye than to overbake and end up with hard, dry cupcakes.

And finally, enjoy the process! Baking is about experimenting, learning, sharing, and taking part in a tradition and passion that has fueled the fire of creativity of bakers and decorators for hundreds of years and many more to come.

ESSENTIAL TOOLS

The tools used in any trade are essential and make a difference in the quality of the work done. There are a few important tools that you will need to make sure you have on hand before you begin the art of cupcake making.

Muffin tins: Muffin tins come in all different shapes and sizes, from mini to jumbo.

Paper liners: Today there are many different types and sizes of cupcake liners to choose from. Colors may vary from white to hot pink with polka dots. If you are using a patterned liner, be sure to use a vanilla-based cupcake so the pattern will still be visible when the cupcake is baked. Check the size of your liner before you start filling your cupcakes, and make sure you don't over- or underfill them. Finally, think about how the liner you are using will affect the overall appearance and presentation of your cupcakes.

Ice cream scoop: A mechanical ice cream scoop is a great tool for filling cupcake liners with batter. It will make uniform scoops, which help the cupcakes bake evenly.

Toothpicks: Toothpicks are an easy way to determine if the center of a cupcake is done. Most often touch the top of the cupcake with my finger to ensure that the cupcake is completely done, but there are times that using a toothpick is best. When the toothpick is inserted into the center of the cupcake and comes out clean or with only a few crumbs, the cupcake is done.

Cooling rack: As the name implies, this tool is perfect for cooling baked goods, allowing the air to circulate quickly and evenly.

Oven thermometer: Oven temperatures vary and can be inaccurate. Using an oven thermometer allows you to monitor the temperature of your oven and to adjust it as needed.

FILLING CUPCAKE CUPS

A medium-sized ice cream scoop is the perfect tool for filling cupcake liners. Each cupcake is measured perfectly, and there is very little mess. The cupcake liners should be ¾ full.

1. Fill scoop completely full; do not over- or underfill.
2. Release batter into the center of the liner.
3. Tap baking tin on counter to settle batter before baking.

ICING THE CUPCAKES

Cupcakes can be iced in a variety of ways. A large round or star tip is the easiest way to quickly ice a cupcake.

1. Hold bag at a 90-degree angle and place tip above the center of the cupcake.
2. Begin squeezing with even pressure as you swirl the icing clockwise, creating a thick layer of icing.
3. Stop squeezing when tip has returned to center of cupcake. Release pressure and lift up, creating a center peak.

TOOLS FOR ICING AND DECORATING

Pastry bag: A pastry bag is essential to icing uniformed cupcakes. It gives you control, keeps your hands clean, and will give your cupcakes a professional look. Disposable bags are easy to use and make the clean up simple.

Offset spatula: This is also known as an icing spatula. A small offset spatula is perfect for hand icing cupcakes or for creating a rustic natural look for the top of your cupcakes.

Gel-paste colors: More concentrated than liquid coloring, they are the perfect choice for tinting icings and fondant. Only a few drops are generally needed, and they are available in a large variety of colors. They are inexpensive, easy to find, and will last a long time.

X-Acto knife: The tiny blade on this knife makes it perfect for cutting out shapes, getting into hard to reach places, and creating clean, precise cuts to fondant decorations.

Small rolling pin: Ideal for rolling out small amounts of fondant.

Small paintbrush: Used to attach candies and fondant, and perfect for applying gel colors and touching up mistakes.

Sprinkles and candies: The perfect adornment for themed cupcakes, sprinkles and candies help add color texture without altering the taste of the cupcakes.

Fondant: A soft, pliable sugar icing, fondant has the texture of play dough and has only the limitation of your imagination. It needs to be used at room temperature and must be kneaded before it's used. It can be colored, flavored, rolled, thinned, cut, pulled, molded, and dried to create any type of design. It has a light marshmallow taste and can be purchased or made.

Piping tips: To create the look of the cupcakes in this book, you will need a medium to large round tip and a medium to large star tip. Each brand of tip is numbered to make the ordering and replacement easier. We use Ateco number 829 and Wilton number 809. Like the name, the round tips create a clean round edge, while the star tip is beveled and creates raised edges on the icing.

Spring

COCONUT CREAM
cupcakes

Buttery coconut cake filled with homemade coconut pastry cream and topped with light coconut cream cheese and toasted coconut makes this cupcake paradise for coconut flavors.

Makes
24
cupcakes

WET INGREDIENTS

¼ cup unsalted butter, softened

3 large eggs

½ cup sour cream

¼ cup unsweetened applesauce

½ cup vegetable oil

2 Tbsp. pure vanilla

1 tsp. coconut extract

⅔ cup coconut milk

DRY INGREDIENTS

1 cup sugar

2 cups flour

½ cup sweetened flake coconut

1¼ Tbsp. baking powder

½ tsp. salt

1. Preheat oven to 350 degrees.

2. Beat butter and sugar on medium speed in the bowl of a stand mixer, using the paddle attachment, until smooth. Stop the mixer and scrape down the sides of the bowl. Add eggs one at a time, beating well after each addition. Beat in sour cream, applesauce, oil, vanilla, and coconut extract. Mix until ingredients are well-blended and smooth.

3. In a separate bowl, sift flour, coconut, baking powder, and salt. Beat ⅓ of the flour mixture into wet ingredients. Alternatively add flour mixture and coconut milk to wet ingredients, blending until smooth.

4. Line two standard muffin tins with paper cupcake liners. Fill each cup ⅔ full with batter. I like to use an ice cream scoop for perfect measuring every time! Bake until tops spring back to the touch, and edges are just golden brown, 20–22 minutes.

5. Remove from tins and cool completely before filling or icing.

Finishing Touches: Core the center of the cupcake using a teaspoon. Fill with Toasted Coconut Cream Filling (126), top with Whipped Cream Frosting (108), and garnish with Toasted Coconut (126).

Brown

RASPBERRY LIME
cupcakes

Makes
24
cupcakes

Fresh raspberry Purée marbles this light key lime cake, making it an instant favorite. The center is filled with raspberry lime curd, packing it full of flavor.

WET INGREDIENTS

½ cup unsalted butter, softened

zest of 4 Key limes

¼ cup milk

3 large eggs

2 Tbsp. pure vanilla

½ cup fresh lime juice

DRY INGREDIENTS

1½ cups sugar

2½ cups flour

½ tsp. salt

2 Tbsp. baking powder

1. Preheat oven to 350 degrees.

2. Beat butter and sugar at medium speed in the bowl of a stand mixer with the paddle attachment until smooth. Stop mixer and scrape down the sides of the bowl. Add lime zest, milk, eggs, and vanilla. Mix until ingredients are well blended and smooth.

3. In a separate bowl, sift dry ingredients. Turn the stand mixer onto low, add dry ingredients, and mix until just incorporated. Batter should be smooth. Add lime juice last and mix until smooth.

4. Line two standard muffin tins with paper cupcake liners. Fill each cup ⅔ full with batter. I like to use an ice cream scoop for perfect measuring every time! Bake until tops spring back at the touch of your finger, and edges are just starting to brown, 20–22 minutes.

5. Remove from tins and cool completely before filling and icing.

Finishing Touches: Core the center of the cupcakes and fill with Raspberry Lime Curd (127). Ice with Raspberry Lime Cream Icing (120) and garnish with a raspberry or lime wedge.

Note: If the baking powder is not sifted with the dry ingredients it will begin to react with the citric acid and the batter will begin to bubble and quickly rise.

Brown

TANGERINE
cupcakes

Just the name of this cupcake sounds light and refreshing. Fresh tangerine juice and zest from the peel will leave you feeling rejuvenated and hungry for more.

WET INGREDIENTS

½ cup unsalted butter, softened

½ cup fresh squeezed tangerine juice

zest of 4 tangerines

¼ cup milk

3 large eggs

1 Tbsp. orange extract

1 Tbsp. pure vanilla

DRY INGREDIENTS

1½ cups sugar

4 Tbsp. brown sugar

2½ cups flour

½ tsp. salt

2 Tbsp. baking powder

1. Preheat oven to 350 degrees.

2. Beat butter and sugar at medium speed in the bowl of a stand mixer with the paddle attachment until smooth. Stop mixer and scrape down the sides of the bowl. Add tangerine juice, zest, milk, eggs, orange extract, and vanilla. Mix until ingredients are well blended and smooth.

3. In a separate bowl, sift dry ingredients. Turn the stand mixer onto low, add dry ingredients, and mix until just incorporated. Batter should be smooth.

4. Line two standard muffin tins with paper cupcake liners. Fill each cup ⅔ full with batter. I like to use an ice cream scoop for perfect measuring every time! Bake until tops spring back at the touch of your finger, and edges are just starting to brown, 20–22 minutes.

5. Remove from tins and cool completely before filling and icing.

Finishing Touches: Ice with Tangerine Buttercream (113) and garnish with tangerine zest.

Note: If the baking powder is not sifted with the dry ingredients it will begin to react with the citric acid and the batter will begin to bubble and quickly rise.

HUMMINGBIRD
cupcakes

Makes
24
cupcakes

This is the perfect cupcake to announce the coming of spring—a South-ern favorite that brings together the flavors of coconut, pineapple, and pecans.

WET INGREDIENTS

½ cup unsalted butter, softened

½ cup sour cream

¼ cup buttermilk

¼ cup unsweetened applesauce

½ cup vegetable oil

3 large eggs

1 Tbsp. pure vanilla

⅔ cup bananas, peeled and mashed

⅔ cup crushed pineapple, drained

⅔ cup shredded coconut

⅔ cup chopped walnuts (optional)

1 pineapple (optional)

DRY INGREDIENTS

1¼ cup brown sugar

2½ cups flour

1¼ Tbsp. baking powder

½ tsp. salt

1 tsp. ground cinnamon

1. Preheat the oven to 350 degrees.

2. Beat butter and sugar at medium speed in the bowl of a stand mixer with the paddle attachment until smooth. Stop mixer and scrape down the sides of the bowl. Add sour cream, buttermilk, applesauce, oil, eggs, and vanilla. Mix until ingredients are well blended and smooth.

3. In a separate bowl, sift remaining dry ingredients.

4. Turn the stand mixer onto low and add dry ingredients until just incorporated. The batter should be smooth.

5. Fold in mashed bananas, pineapple, coconut, and nuts. Mix evenly.

6. Line two standard muffin tins with paper cupcake liners. Fill each cup ⅔ full with batter. I like to use an ice cream scoop for perfect measuring every time! Bake until tops spring back to the touch of your finger, and edges are golden brown, 20–22 minutes.

7. Trim all the skin off the pineapple, then cut off the top and the bottom of the pineapple. Cut the pineapple into really thin circle-shaped slices. Grease a cupcake pan with no stick spray, and press pineapple slices down into the bottom of the cupcake tins like cupcake liners. Stick pan in the oven and bake at 170 degrees for about 3 hours to dry the pineapple circles or until they are slightly brown.

8. Remove cup from tins and cool completely before filling or icing.

Finishing Touches: Ice with Cream Cheese Icing (108) and garnish with a dried slice of pineapple.

Brown

TRES LECHE
cupcakes

Makes
24
cupcakes

A Mexican tradition has made this cake famous across the world! Vanilla bean cake soaked in three different types of milk, layered with fresh strawberries, and topped with fresh whipped cream will make it an instant tradition for your family as well.

WET INGREDIENTS

¼ cup unsalted butter, softened

½ cup sour cream

¼ cup buttermilk

¼ cup unsweetened applesauce

½ cup vegetable oil

3 large eggs

2 Tbsp. pure vanilla

DRY INGREDIENTS

1 cup sugar

2 cups flour

1¼ Tbsp. baking powder

½ tsp. salt

2 tsp. cinnamon

1 Three-Milk Recipe (132)

1. Preheat the oven to 350 degrees.

2. Beat butter and sugar at medium speed in the bowl of a stand mixer with the paddle attachment until smooth. Stop mixer and scrape down the sides of the bowl. Add sour cream, buttermilk, applesauce, oil, eggs, and vanilla. Mix until ingredients are well blended and smooth.

3. In a separate bowl, sift flour, baking powder, salt, and cinnamon.

4. Turn the stand mixer onto low and add dry ingredients until just incorporated. The batter should be smooth.

5. Line two standard muffin tins with paper cupcake liners. Fill each cup ⅔ full with batter. I like to use an ice cream scoop for perfect measuring every time! Bake until tops spring back to the touch of your finger, and edges are just golden brown, 20–25 minutes.

6. Remove from tins and cool completely before filling or icing.

7. Using a fork, poke numerous holes in the top of cupcake. Using a spoon, pour three-milk mixture over cupcakes until milk mixture has been absorbed.

Finishing Touches: Ice with Whipped Cream Cheese Icing (108) and garnish with caramel.

STRAWBERRY RHUBARB *cupcakes*

Makes
24
cupcakes

Rhubarb always reminds me of my grandma Randall. She had the most creative recipes for using it. I like it best when paired with fresh strawberries and hope you do too!

WET INGREDIENTS

¼ cup unsalted butter, softened

½ cup sour cream

¼ cup orange juice

¼ cup unsweetened applesauce

½ cup vegetable oil

3 large eggs

2 Tbsp. pure vanilla

1½ cups chopped strawberries

½ cup finely chopped rhubarb

DRY INGREDIENTS

1 cup sugar

2 cups flour

1¼ Tbsp. baking powder

½ tsp. salt

1. Preheat the oven to 350 degrees.

2. Beat butter and sugar at medium speed in the bowl of a stand mixer with the paddle attachment until smooth. Stop mixer and scrape down the sides of the bowl. Add sour cream, orange juice, applesauce, oil, eggs, and vanilla. Mix until ingredients are well blended and smooth.

3. In a separate bowl, sift flour, baking powder, and salt.

4. Turn the stand mixer onto low and add dry ingredients until just incorporated. The batter should be smooth. Fold in chopped strawberries and rhubarb.

5. Line two standard muffin tins with paper cupcake liners. Fill each cup ⅔ full with batter. I like to use an ice cream scoop for perfect measuring every time! Bake until the tops spring back to the touch of your finger, and the edges are just golden brown, 20–22 minutes.

6. Remove from tins and cool completely before filling or icing

Finishing Touches: Ice with Lemon Whipped Cream Cheese Icing (108) and garnish with a sliced strawberry.

Brown

COCONUT LEMON
cupcakes

Makes
24
cupcakes

This is the uniting of two spring favorites. The result is light, refreshing, and definitely unique.

WET INGREDIENTS

½ cup unsalted butter, softened

½ cup fresh lemon juice

zest of 3 lemons

¼ cup milk

3 large eggs

1 Tbsp. coconut extract

2 Tbsp. pure vanilla

DRY INGREDIENTS

1½ cups sugar

2½ cups flour

½ tsp. salt

2 Tbsp. baking powder

1 cup coconut flakes

1. Preheat oven to 350 degrees.

2. Beat butter and sugar at medium speed in the bowl of a stand mixer with the paddle attachment until smooth. Stop mixer and scrape down the sides of the bowl. Add lemon juice and zest, milk, eggs, coconut extract, and vanilla. Mix until ingredients are well blended and smooth.

3. In a separate bowl, sift dry ingredients. Turn the stand mixer onto low, add dry ingredients, and mix until just incorporated. Batter should be smooth.

4. Line two standard muffin tins with paper cupcake liners. Fill each cup ⅔ full with batter. I like to use an ice cream scoop for perfect measuring every time! Bake until the tops spring back at the touch of your finger, and the edges are just starting to brown, 20–25 minutes.

5. Remove from tins and cool completely before filling and icing.

Finishing Touches: Core center of cupcake and fill with Lemon Cream (127). Ice with Coconut Cream Cheese (110) and garnish with Lemon Heads and coconut flakes.

Brown

ORANGE CREAM
cupcakes

The best part of this cupcake is the center. Peel back layers of orange blossom cake, lick away homemade orange cream cheese, and get down to eating the smooth cream filling at the center.

Makes
24
cupcakes

WET INGREDIENTS

¼ cup unsalted butter, softened

2 Tbsp. orange zest

½ cup sour cream

¼ cup buttermilk

¼ cup orange juice

¼ cup unsweetened applesauce

½ cup vegetable oil

3 large eggs

2 Tbsp. pure vanilla

DRY INGREDIENTS

1 cup sugar

2 cups flour

1¼ Tbsp. baking powder

½ tsp. salt

1. Preheat the oven to 350 degrees.

2. Beat butter and sugar at medium speed in the bowl of a stand mixer with the paddle attachment until smooth. Stop mixer and scrape down the sides of the bowl. Add sour cream, buttermilk, orange juice, zest, applesauce, oil, eggs, and vanilla. Mix until ingredients are well blended and smooth.

3. In a separate bowl, sift flour, baking powder, and salt.

4. Turn the stand mixer onto low and add dry ingredients until just incorporated. The batter should be smooth.

5. Line two standard muffin tins with paper cupcake liners. Fill each cup ⅔ full with batter. I like to use an ice cream scoop for perfect measuring every time! Bake until tops spring back to the touch of your finger, and edges are just golden brown, 20–25 minutes.

6. Remove from tins and cool completely before filling or icing.

Finishing Touches: Core center of cupcake and fill with Cream Filling (128). Ice with Orange Cream Cheese (110) and garnish with non perils (sprinkles).

CHOCOLATE BLACKBERRY *cupcakes*

Dark chocolate cake marbled with fresh blackberry purée and topped with a healthy dose of blackberry buttercream will make you wish it was spring all year long.

Makes
24
cupcakes

WET INGREDIENTS

½ cup dark chocolate, chopped into small pieces

½ cup boiling water

½ cup sour cream

½ cup unsweetened applesauce

½ cup vegetable oil

3 large eggs

1 Tbsp. pure vanilla

½ cup Blackberry Purée (128)

DRY INGREDIENTS

½ cup Dutch-process cocoa powder

1½ cups flour

1 cup sugar

1 Tbsp. baking powder

½ tsp. salt

1. Preheat oven to 350 degrees.

2. Place chocolate in the bowl of a stand mixer. Pour boiling water over chocolate and let sit for 1 minute. Using the whisk attachment mix until smooth. Scrape down the sides of the bowl. Add sour cream, applesauce, oil, cocoa powder, eggs, and vanilla.

3. In a separate bowl, sift flour, sugar, baking powder, and salt.

4. Turn the stand mixer onto low, add dry ingredients, and mix until just incorporated. Batter should be smooth. Add Blackberry Purée to the batter and marble.

5. Line two standard muffin tins with paper cupcake liners. Fill each cup ⅔ full with batter. I like to use an ice cream scoop for perfect measuring every time! Bake until tops spring back to the touch of your finger, and a toothpick inserted into the center comes out clean, 20–25 minutes.

6. Remove from tins and cool completely before filling and icing.

Finishing Touches: Ice with Blackberry Buttercream (114) and garnish with a fresh blackberry.

Brown

CHOCOLATE STRAWBERRY *cupcakes*

This cupcake helped us gain the third spot for best cupcakes in the United States! With chocolate dipped strawberries as the inspiration, there will never be any leftovers.

WET INGREDIENTS

½ cup dark chocolate, chopped into small pieces

½ cup boiling water

½ cup sour cream

½ cup unsweetened applesauce

½ cup vegetable oil

3 large eggs

1 Tbsp. pure vanilla

½ cup Strawberry Purée (128)

DRY INGREDIENTS

½ cup Dutch-process cocoa powder

1½ cups flour

1 cup sugar

1 Tbsp. baking powder

½ tsp. salt

1. Preheat oven to 350 degrees.

2. Place chocolate in the bowl of a stand mixer. Pour boiling water over chocolate and let sit for 1 minute. Using the whisk attachment mix until smooth. Scrape down the sides of the bowl. Add sour cream, applesauce, oil, cocoa powder, eggs, and vanilla.

3. In a separate bowl, sift flour, sugar, baking powder, and salt.

4. Turn the stand mixer onto low, add dry ingredients, and mix until just incorporated. Batter should be smooth. Add Strawberry Purée to the batter and marble.

5. Line two standard muffin tins with paper cupcake liners. Fill each cup ⅔ full with batter. I like to use an ice cream scoop for perfect measuring every time! Bake until tops spring back to the touch of your finger, and a toothpick inserted into the center comes out clean, 20–25 minutes.

6. Remove from tins and cool completely before filling and icing.

Finishing Touches: Core center of cupcakes and fill with remaining Purée and freshly chopped strawberries.

Spread a thick later of Dark Chocolate Ganache (125) over the top of the cupcake. Ice with Strawberry Buttercream (113) and garnish with a fresh strawberry and drizzle with Dark Chocolate Ganache.

BLUEBERRY HONEY
cupcakes

Eating these cupcakes warm with honey cream cheese melting down the sides is the perfect justification for having a cupcake any time of day, breakfast included.

WET INGREDIENTS

¼ cup unsalted butter, softened

½ cup sour cream

¼ cup buttermilk

¼ cup unsweetened applesauce

½ cup vegetable oil

3 large eggs

2 Tbsp. pure vanilla

2 Tbsp. of honey

1 cup fresh blueberries

DRY INGREDIENTS

1 cup sugar

2 cups all-purpose flour

1¼ Tbsp. baking powder

½ tsp. salt

1. Preheat the oven to 350 degrees.

2. Beat butter and sugar at medium speed in the bowl of a stand mixer with the paddle attachment until smooth. Stop mixer and scrape down the sides of the bowl. Add sour cream, buttermilk, applesauce, oil, eggs, vanilla, and honey. Mix until ingredients are well blended and smooth.

3. In a separate bowl, sift flour, baking powder, and salt.

4. Turn the stand mixer onto low and add dry ingredients, except ¼ cup flour, until just incorporated. The batter should be smooth.

5. Rinse blueberries and place in a plastic bag with the extra ¼ cup flour. Seal and shake the bag until blueberries are coated with flour. Fold blueberries into the batter. This will keep the blueberries from sinking to the bottom of the cupcake.

6. Line two standard muffin tins with paper cupcake liners. Fill each cup ⅔ full with batter. I like to use an ice cream scoop for perfect measuring every time! Bake until tops spring back to the touch of your finger, and edges are just golden brown, 20–25 minutes.

7. Remove from tins and cool completely before filling or icing.

Finishing Touches: Ice with Honey Cream Cheese (110) and garnish with a fresh blueberry.

DULCE DE LECHE
cupcakes

Makes
24
cupcakes

Thick, gooey caramel fills the center of this cupcake and is folded into the rich buttercream on top. My favorite part of eating this cupcake is licking the caramel off my fingers!

WET INGREDIENTS

¼ cup unsalted butter, softened

½ cup sour cream

¼ cup buttermilk

¼ cup unsweetened applesauce

½ cup vegetable oil

3 large eggs

2 Tbsp. pure vanilla

1 (12-oz.) can dulce de leche

DRY INGREDIENTS

1 cup brown sugar

2 cups flour

1¼ Tbsp. baking powder

½ tsp. salt

1. Preheat the oven to 350 degrees.

2. Beat butter and sugar at medium speed in the bowl of a stand mixer with the paddle attachment until smooth. Stop mixer and scrape down the sides of the bowl. Add sour cream, buttermilk, applesauce, oil, eggs, and vanilla. Mix until ingredients are well blended and smooth.

3. In a separate bowl, sift flour, baking powder, and salt.

4. Turn the stand mixer onto low and add dry ingredients until just incorporated. The batter should be smooth.

5. Line two standard muffin tins with paper cupcake liners. Fill each cup ⅔ full with batter. I like to use an ice cream scoop for perfect measuring every time! Bake until tops spring back to the touch of your finger, and edges are just golden brown, 20–25 minutes.

6. Remove from tins and cool completely before filling or icing.

7. Core the center of each cupcake and fill with dulce de leche caramel.

Finishing Touches: Ice with Dulce de Leche Icing (120).

HONEY BUN
cupcakes

Served warm, this cupcake will melt in your mouth! Ground cinnamon, honey, and delicious cream cheese create the perfect combination.

Makes
24
cupcakes

WET INGREDIENTS

¼ cup unsalted butter, softened

½ cup sour cream

¼ cup buttermilk

¼ cup unsweetened applesauce

½ cup vegetable oil

3 large eggs

2 Tbsp. pure vanilla

1 Tbsp. vanilla bean paste

¼ cup honey

¼ cup cinnamon

¼ cup melted butter

DRY INGREDIENTS

1 cup sugar

2 cups flour

1¼ Tbsp. baking powder

½ tsp. salt

1. Preheat the oven to 350 degrees.

2. Beat butter and sugar at medium speed in the bowl of a stand mixer with the paddle attachment until smooth. Stop mixer and scrape down the sides of the bowl. Add sour cream, buttermilk, applesauce, oil, eggs, vanilla, and vanilla bean paste. Mix until ingredients are well blended and smooth.

3. In a separate bowl sift flour, baking powder, and salt.

4. Turn the stand mixer onto low and add dry ingredients until just incorporated. The batter should be smooth.

5. In a small separate bowl, combine honey, cinnamon, and melted butter. Stir until smooth. Fold into cupcake batter until marbled.

6. Line two standard muffin tins with paper cupcake liners. Fill each cup ⅔ full with batter. I like to use an ice cream scoop for perfect measuring every time! Bake until tops spring back to the touch of your finger, and edges are just golden brown, 20–25 minutes.

7. Remove from tins and cool completely before filling or icing.

Finishing Touches: Drizzle with Cream Cheese Honey Glaze (110).

Brown

Summer

ROOT BEER FLOAT
cupcakes

Makes
24
cupcakes

This is a fan favorite. Moist root beer cake topped with a scoop of vanilla bean buttercream brings back summer memories in every bite.

WET INGREDIENTS

¼ cup unsalted butter, softened

½ cup sour cream

¼ cup root beer

¼ cup unsweetened applesauce

½ cup vegetable oil

3 large eggs

2 Tbsp. pure vanilla

2 Tbsp. root beer extract

DRY INGREDIENTS

2 cups flour

1 cup sugar

1¼ Tbsp. baking powder

½ tsp. salt

1. Preheat the oven to 350 degrees.

2. Beat butter and sugar at medium speed in the bowl of a stand mixer with the paddle attachment until smooth. Stop mixer and scrape down the sides of the bowl. Add sour cream, Root Beer, applesauce, oil, eggs, vanilla, and Root Beer extract. Mix until ingredients are well blended and smooth.

3. In a separate bowl, sift flour, baking powder, and salt.

4. Turn the stand mixer onto low and add dry ingredients until just incorporated. The batter should be smooth.

5. Line two standard muffin tins with paper cupcake liners. Fill each cup ⅔ full with batter. I like to use an ice cream scoop for perfect measuring every time! Bake until tops spring back to the touch of your finger, and edges are just golden brown, 20–25 minutes.

6. Remove from tins and cool completely before filling or icing.

Finishing Touches: Ice with Vanilla Bean Buttercream (113).

CHERRY COKE FLOAT
cupcakes

Now you can have your favorite drink in cupcake form! This chocolate cherry Coke creation has become a classic.

Makes
24
cupcakes

WET INGREDIENTS

½ cup dark chocolate
chopped into small pieces

½ cup boiling coke

½ cup sour cream

½ cup unsweetened applesauce

½ cup vegetable oil

3 large eggs

1 Tbsp. pure vanilla

DRY INGREDIENTS

1½ cups flour

1 cup sugar

1 Tbsp. baking powder

½ tsp. salt

½ cup Dutch-process cocoa
powder

1 small can cherry pie filling

1. Preheat oven to 350 degrees.

2. Place chocolate in the bowl of a stand mixer. Pour boiling coke over chocolate and let sit for 1 minute. Using the whisk attachment, mix until smooth. Stop mixer and scrape down the sides of the bowl. Add sour cream, applesauce, oil, eggs, and vanilla. Mix until ingredients are well blended and smooth.

3. In a separate bowl, sift flour, sugar, baking powder, salt, and cocoa.

4. Turn the stand mixer onto low, add dry ingredients, and mix until just incorporated. Batter should be smooth.

5. Line two standard muffin tins with paper cupcake liners. Fill each cup ⅔ full with batter. I like to use an ice cream scoop for perfect measuring every time! Bake until tops spring back to the touch of your finger, and a toothpick inserted into the center comes out clean, 22–25 minutes.

6. Remove from tins and cool completely before filling and icing.

Finishing Touches: Core center of cupcakes and fill with cherry pie filling. Apply a thin layer of Cherry Coke Glaze (121) and top with Whipped Cream Cheese Icing (108).

PINK LEMONADE
cupcakes

Nothing says summer like a cold glass of lemonade. This cupcake is the perfect match for a hot summer day.

Makes
24
cupcakes

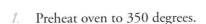

WET INGREDIENTS

½ cup unsalted butter, softened

½ cup fresh lemon juice

zest of 3 lemons

¼ cup milk

3 large eggs

½ cup maraschino cherry juice

2 Tbsp. pure vanilla

DRY INGREDIENTS

1½ cups sugar

2½ cups flour

½ tsp. salt

2 Tbsp. baking powder

1. Preheat oven to 350 degrees.

2. Beat butter and sugar at medium speed in the bowl of a stand mixer with the paddle attachment until smooth. Stop mixer and scrape down the sides of the bowl. Add lemon juice, zest, milk, eggs, maraschino juice, and vanilla. Mix until ingredients are well blended and smooth.

3. In a separate bowl, sift dry ingredients. Turn the stand mixer onto low, add dry ingredients, and mix until just incorporated. Batter should be smooth.

4. Line two standard muffin tins with paper cupcake liners. Fill each cup ⅔ full with batter. I like to use an ice cream scoop for perfect measuring every time! Bake until tops spring back at the touch of your finger, and edges are just starting to brown, 20–25 minutes.

5. Remove from tins and cool completely before filling and icing.

Finishing Touches: Core center of cupcake and fill with Lemon Cream (127). Ice with Pink Lemon Cream Cheese (110) and garnish with Lemon Heads and a straw.

Note: This batter needs time to rest before baking. For best results, let the batter sit refrigerated for at least 30 minutes or overnight before using.

Brown

NEAPOLITAN
cupcakes

Makes
24
cupcakes

Layers of chocolate, vanilla, and strawberry make this cupcake a favorite for everyone. Delicious.

WET INGREDIENTS

¼ cup unsalted butter, softened

¼ cup sour cream

4 Tbsp. buttermilk

4 Tbsp. unsweetened applesauce

¼ cup vegetable oil

1 large egg, plus 1 egg yolk

1 Tbsp. pure vanilla

½ Tbsp. vanilla bean paste

DRY INGREDIENTS

½ cup sugar

1 cups flour

¾ Tbsp. baking powder

¼ tsp. salt

VANILLA BEAN CUPCAKE BATTER

1. Preheat the oven to 350 degrees.

2. Beat butter and sugar at medium speed in the bowl of a stand mixer with the paddle attachment until smooth. Stop mixer and scrape down the sides of the bowl. Add sour cream, buttermilk, applesauce, oil, eggs, vanilla, and vanilla bean paste. Mix until ingredients are well blended and smooth.

3. In a separate bowl, sift flour, baking powder, and salt.

4. Turn the stand mixer onto low and add dry ingredients until just incorporated. The batter should be smooth.

Brown

WET INGREDIENTS

¼ cup dark chocolate
chopped into small pieces

¼ cup boiling water

¼ cup sour cream

¼ cup unsweetened applesauce

¼ cup vegetable oil

1 large egg, plus 1 egg yolk

½ Tbsp. pure vanilla

DRY INGREDIENTS

¾ cup flour

½ cup sugar

½ Tbsp. baking powder

¼ tsp. salt

¼ cup Dutch-process
cocoa powder

UNBEATABLE CHOCOLATE CUPCAKE BATTER

1. Place chocolate in the bowl of a stand mixer. Pour boiling water over chocolate and let sit for 1 minute. Using the whisk attachment, mix until smooth. Scrape down the sides of the bowl. Add sour cream, applesauce, oil, eggs, and vanilla. Mix until ingredients are well blended and smooth.

2. In a separate bowl, sift flour, sugar, baking powder, salt, and cocoa powder.

3. Turn the stand mixer onto low, add dry ingredients, and mix until just incorporated. Batter should be smooth.

4. Line two standard muffin tins with paper cupcake liners. Fill each cup one third full with chocolate batter and one third full of vanilla bean batter. Be careful not to over fill. I like to use an ice cream scoop for perfect measuring every time! Bake until tops spring back to the touch of your finger, and a toothpick inserted into the center comes out clean, 20–25 minutes.

5. Remove from tins and cool completely before filling and icing.

Finishing Touches: Ice with Strawberry Buttercream (113) and garnish with a fresh strawberry and Dark Chocolate Ganache (125).

Note: Be careful not to overfill your cupcake liners! These cupcakes will crown nicely, but if overfilled the batter will spill over and create a "pocket" on the side of your cupcake.

BANANA SPLIT
cupcakes

Makes
24
cupcakes

America's favorite ice cream dish now comes in cupcake form! Eat each flavor individually or ice one cupcake with all three flavors to experience dessert at its best.

WET INGREDIENTS

½ cup unsalted butter, softened

½ cup sour cream

¼ cup buttermilk

¼ cup unsweetened applesauce

½ cup vegetable oil

4 large eggs

1 Tbsp. pure vanilla

4 ripe bananas, peeled and mashed

DRY INGREDIENTS

1¼ cup brown sugar

2½ cups flour

1¼ Tbsp. baking powder

½ tsp. salt

1 tsp. ground cinnamon

1. Preheat the oven to 350 degrees.

2. Beat butter and sugar at medium speed in the bowl of a stand mixer with the paddle attachment until smooth. Stop mixer and scrape down the sides of the bowl. Add sour cream, buttermilk, applesauce, oil, eggs, vanilla, and mashed bananas. Mix until ingredients are well blended and smooth.

3. In a separate bowl, sift flour, baking powder, salt, and cinnamon.

4. Turn the stand mixer onto low and add the dry ingredients until just incorporated. The batter should be smooth.

5. Line two standard muffin tins with paper cupcake liners. Fill each cup ⅔ full with batter. I like to use an ice cream scoop for perfect measuring every time! Bake until tops spring back to the touch of your finger, and edges are just golden brown, 20–25 minutes.

6. Remove from tins and cool completely before filling or icing.

Finishing Touches: Ice with Chocolate, Strawberry, and Vanilla Bean Buttercream (111, 113). Drizzle with Dark Chocolate Ganache (125) and garnish with sprinkles and a cherry.

Summer

COOKIE DOUGH
cupcakes

Makes
24
cupcakes

Nothing brings back childhood memories like eating cookie dough! This recipe combines an egg-less chocolate chip cookie dough with vanilla bean cake and cream cheese icing. You'll need a glass of milk before you're done!

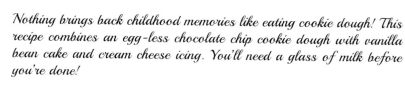

WET INGREDIENTS

¼ cup unsalted butter, softened

½ cup sour cream

¼ cup buttermilk

¼ cup unsweetened applesauce

½ cup vegetable oil

3 large eggs

2 Tbsp. pure vanilla

1 Tbsp. vanilla bean paste

DRY INGREDIENTS

1 cup sugar

2 cups flour

1¼ Tbsp. baking powder

½ tsp. salt

1. Preheat the oven to 350 degrees.

2. Beat butter and sugar at medium speed in the bowl of a stand mixer with the paddle attachment until smooth. Stop mixer and scrape down the sides of the bowl. Add sour cream, buttermilk, applesauce, oil, eggs, vanilla, and vanilla bean paste. Mix until ingredients are well blended and smooth.

3. In a separate bowl, sift flour, baking powder, and salt.

4. Turn the stand mixer onto low and add dry ingredients until just incorporated. The batter should be smooth.

5. Line two standard muffin tins with paper cupcake liners. Fill each cup half full with batter. Drop a small scoop of Egg-less Chocolate Chip Cookie Dough (131) into the center of the cupcake batter and press the dough down until it almost touches the bottom of the liner. Bake until tops spring back to the touch of your finger, and edges are just golden brown, 20–25 minutes.

6. Remove from tins and cool completely before filling or icing.

Finishing Touches: Ice with Cream Cheese Icing (110) and garnish with chocolate chips.

Summer

CHOCOLATE MALTED MILK *cupcakes*

Makes
24
cupcakes

Malted milk balls top this cupcake making it a dessert with a dessert.

WET INGREDIENTS

½ cup dark chocolate
chopped into small pieces

½ cup boiling water

½ cup sour cream

½ cup unsweetened applesauce

½ cup vegetable oil

3 large eggs

1 Tbsp. pure vanilla

DRY INGREDIENTS

1½ cups flour

1 cup sugar

1 Tbsp. baking powder

½ tsp. salt

½ cup Dutch-process cocoa
powder

1 cup malted milk

1. Preheat oven to 350 degrees.

2. Place chocolate in the bowl of a stand mixer. Pour boiling water over chocolate and let sit for 1 minute. Using the whisk attachment mix until smooth. Scrape down the sides of the bowl. Add sour cream, applesauce, oil, eggs, and vanilla. Mix until ingredients are well blended and smooth.

3. In a separate bowl, sift flour, sugar, baking powder, salt, cocoa, and malted milk.

4. Turn the stand mixer onto low, add dry ingredients, and mix until just incorporated. Batter should be smooth.

5. Line two standard muffin tins with paper cupcake liners. Fill each cup ⅔ full with batter. I like to use an ice cream scoop for perfect measuring every time! Bake until tops spring back to the touch of your finger, and a toothpick inserted into the center comes out clean, 22–25 minutes.

6. Remove from tins and cool completely before filling and icing.

Finishing Touches: Ice with Chocolate Malt Buttercream (119), and garnish with a chocolate malt ball.

BUMBLEBEE
cupcakes

Makes
24
cupcakes

My favorite birthday cake flavor growing up, this cupcake reflects a timeless tradition of perfect yellow cake with thick chocolate ganache icing. It will make you smile.

WET INGREDIENTS

¼ cup unsalted butter, softened

½ cup sour cream

¼ cup buttermilk

¼ cup unsweetened applesauce

½ cup vegetable oil

2 large eggs plus 2 egg yolks

2 Tbsp. pure vanilla

DRY INGREDIENTS

1 cup sugar

2 cups flour

1¼ Tbsp. baking powder

½ tsp. salt

1. Preheat the oven to 350 degrees.

2. Beat butter and sugar at medium speed in the bowl of a stand mixer with the paddle attachment until smooth. Stop mixer and scrape down the sides of the bowl. Add sour cream, buttermilk, applesauce, oil, eggs, yolks, and vanilla. Mix until ingredients are well blended and smooth.

3. In a separate bowl, sift the flour, baking powder, and salt.

4. Turn the stand mixer onto low and add dry ingredients until just incorporated. The batter should be smooth.

5. Line two standard muffin tins with paper cupcake liners. Fill each cup ⅔ full with batter. I like to use an ice cream scoop for perfect measuring every time! Bake until tops spring back to the touch of your finger, and edges are just golden brown, 20–25 minutes.

6. Remove from tins and cool completely before filling or icing.

Finishing Touches: Ice with Chocolate Ganache (125).

Brown

CHOCOLATE MUD
cupcakes

Makes
24
cupcakes

This is the cupcake that every chocolate lover dreams of eating. Indulge in layers of chocolate and flavor.

WET INGREDIENTS

½ cup dark chocolate chopped into small pieces

½ cup boiling water

½ cup sour cream

½ cup unsweetened applesauce

½ cup vegetable oil

3 large eggs

1 Tbsp. pure vanilla

1 Tbsp. coffee extract

DRY INGREDIENTS

1½ cups flour

1 cup sugar

1 Tbsp. baking powder

½ tsp. salt

½ cup Dutch-process cocoa powder

2 tsp. instant coffee powder

1. Preheat oven to 350 degrees.

2. Place chocolate in the bowl of a stand mixer. Pour boiling water over chocolate and let sit for 1 minute. Using the whisk attachment, mix until smooth. Scrape down the sides of the bowl. Add sour cream, applesauce, oil, eggs, vanilla, and coffee extract. Mix until ingredients are well blended and smooth.

3. In a separate bowl, sift flour, sugar, baking powder, salt, cocoa, and instant coffee powder.

4. Turn the stand mixer onto low, add dry ingredients, and mix until just incorporated. Batter should be smooth.

5. Line two standard muffin tins with paper cupcake liners. Fill each cup ⅔ full with batter. I like to use an ice cream scoop for perfect measuring every time! Bake until tops spring back to the touch of your finger, and a toothpick inserted into the center comes out clean, 22–25 minutes.

6. Remove from tins and cool completely before filling and icing.

Finishing Touches: Layer with Dark Chocolate Ganache (125) and ice with Chocolate Buttercream (111). Garnish with crushed pecans.

Summer

PINEAPPLE MANGO
cupcakes

Makes
24
cupcakes

One bite of this cupcake will send you on a tropical get away. Juicy pineapple and sweet mangos create a flavor experience you won't forget.

WET INGREDIENTS

¼ cup unsalted butter, softened

¼ cup sour cream

¼ cup buttermilk

½ cup vegetable oil

3 large eggs

2 Tbsp. pure vanilla

1 (20-oz.) can crushed pineapple, puréed

DRY INGREDIENTS

1 cup sugar

2½ cups flour

1¼ Tbsp. baking powder

½ tsp. salt

1. Preheat the oven to 350 degrees.

2. Beat butter and sugar at medium speed in the bowl of a stand mixer with the paddle attachment until smooth. Stop mixer and scrape down the sides of the bowl. Add sour cream, buttermilk, oil, eggs, and vanilla. Mix until ingredients are well blended and smooth.

3. In a separate bowl, sift the flour, baking powder, and salt.

4. Turn the stand mixer onto low and add the dry ingredients until just incorporated. The batter should be smooth. Fold in pineapple and mix until smooth.

5. Line two standard muffin tins with paper cupcake liners. Fill each cup ⅔ full with batter. I like to use an ice cream scoop for perfect measuring every time! Bake until tops spring back to the touch of your finger, and edges are just golden brown, about 20–25 minutes.

6. Remove from tins and cool completely before filling or icing.

Finishing Touches: Ice with Mango Buttercream (114).

Brown

STRAWBERRY BANANA *cupcakes*

Makes
24
cupcakes

Moist banana cupcakes swirled with strawberry preserves and straw-berry buttercream make up this fun and fruity cupcake.

WET INGREDIENTS

½ cup unsalted butter, softened

½ cup sour cream

¼ cup buttermilk

¼ cup unsweetened applesauce

½ cup vegetable oil

4 large eggs

1 Tbsp. pure vanilla

4 ripe bananas, peeled and mashed

½ cup Strawberry Purée (128)

DRY INGREDIENTS

1¼ cup brown sugar

2½ cups flour

1¼ Tbsp. baking powder

½ tsp. salt

1. Preheat the oven to 350 degrees.

2. Beat butter and sugar at medium speed in the bowl of a stand mixer with the paddle attachment until smooth. Stop mixer and scrape down the sides of the bowl. Add sour cream, buttermilk, applesauce, oil, eggs, vanilla, and mashed bananas. Mix until ingredients are well blended and smooth.

3. In a separate bowl, sift the flour, baking powder, and salt.

4. Turn the stand mixer onto low and add the dry ingredients until just incorporated. The batter should be smooth. Fold in Strawberry Purée and stir until marbled.

5. Line two standard muffin tins with paper cupcake liners. Fill each cup ⅔ full with batter. I like to use an ice cream scoop for perfect measuring every time! Bake until tops spring back to the touch of your finger, and edges are just golden brown, 20–25 minutes.

6. Remove from tins and cool completely before filling or icing.

Finishing Touches: Core center of cupcakes and fill with Strawberry Filling (131). Ice with Strawberry Buttercream (113) and garnish with a strawberry.

Summer

WATERMELON LIME
cupcakes

Squeezing a fresh lime wedge onto a slice of watermelon is a Southern favorite. Why not try it in a cupcake?

Makes
24
cupcakes

WET INGREDIENTS

½ cup unsalted butter, softened

½ cup fresh lime juice

zest of 4 Key limes

¼ cup milk

3 large eggs

2 Tbsp. pure vanilla

1 Tbsp. coconut extract

DRY INGREDIENTS

1½ cups sugar

2½ cups flour

½ tsp. salt

2 Tbsp. baking powder

1. Preheat oven to 350 degrees.

2. Beat butter and sugar at medium speed in the bowl of a stand mixer with the paddle attachment until smooth. Stop mixer and scrape down the sides of the bowl. Add lime juice, zest, milk, eggs, vanilla, and coconut extract. Mix until ingredients are well blended and smooth.

3. In a separate bowl, sift dry ingredients. Turn the stand mixer onto low, add dry ingredients, and mix until just incorporated. Batter should be smooth.

4. Line two standard muffin tins with paper cupcake liners. Fill each cup ⅔ full with batter. I like to use an ice cream scoop for perfect measuring every time! Bake until tops spring back at the touch of your finger, and edges are just starting to brown, 20–25 minutes.

5. Remove from tins and cool completely before filling and icing.

Finishing Touches: Core the center of the cupcake and fill with Lime Curd (126). Ice with Watermelon Buttercream (116) and garnish with lime zest and a pinch of salt.

Note: If the baking powder is not sifted with the dry ingredients, it will begin to react with the citric acid and the batter will begin to bubble and quickly rise.

Summer

SHIRLEY TEMPLE
cupcakes

This cupcake blends the unique flavors of ginger pomegranate and mar-aschino cherries. One bite will keep you coming back for more.

Makes
24
cupcakes

WET INGREDIENTS

¼ cup unsalted butter, softened

½ cup sour cream

¼ cup ginger ale

¼ cup unsweetened applesauce

½ cup vegetable oil

3 large eggs

2 Tbsp. pure vanilla

½ cup grenadine syrup

DRY INGREDIENTS

1 cup sugar

2 cups flour

1¼ Tbsp. baking powder

½ tsp. salt

⅛ tsp. ginger

1. Preheat the oven to 350 degrees.

2. Beat butter and sugar at medium speed in the bowl of a stand mixer with the paddle attachment until smooth. Stop mixer and scrape down the sides of the bowl. Add sour cream, ginger ale, applesauce, oil, eggs, vanilla, and grenadine syrup. Mix until ingredients are well blended and smooth.

3. In a separate bowl, sift the flour, baking powder, salt, and ginger.

4. Turn the stand mixer onto low and add dry ingredients until just incorporated. The batter should be smooth.

5. Line two standard muffin tins with paper cupcake liners. Fill each cup ⅔ full with batter. I like to use an ice cream scoop for perfect measuring every time! Bake until tops spring back to the touch of your finger, and edges are just golden brown, 20–25 minutes.

6. Remove from tins and cool completely before filling or icing.

Finishing Touches: Ice with Grenadine Buttercream (116) and garnish with a maraschino cherry.

Fall

ZUCCHINI GINGER
cupcakes

My mother makes the most amazing zucchini bread and this is where this recipe originates from. A touch of ginger enhances this moist spice cake and is perfect with a cold glass of milk on a fall evening.

WET INGREDIENTS

3 large eggs

1½ cups vegetable oil

¼ cup orange juice

1 tsp. vanilla extract

¼ cup sour cream

¼ cup applesauce

¼ cup buttermilk

2 cups shredded zucchini

DRY INGREDIENTS

2 cups sugar

3 cups flour

2 tsp. baking powder

1 tsp. baking soda

¾ tsp. ground cinnamon

2 tsp. ground ginger

1 tsp. salt

1. Preheat the oven to 350 degrees.

2. Beat eggs, sugar, oil, orange juice, and vanilla at medium speed in the bowl of a stand mixer with the paddle attachment until smooth. Stop mixer and scrape down the sides of the bowl. Add sour cream, applesauce, and buttermilk. Mix until ingredients are well blended and smooth.

3. In a separate bowl, sift flour, baking powder, baking soda, cinnamon, ginger, and salt.

4. Turn the stand mixer onto low and add dry ingredients until just incorporated. The batter should be smooth. Fold in shredded zucchini until blended.

5. Line two standard muffin tins with paper cupcake liners. Fill each cup ⅔ full with batter. I like to use an ice cream scoop for perfect measuring every time! Bake until tops spring back to the touch of your finger, and edges are just golden brown, 20–25 minutes.

6. Remove from tins and cool completely before icing.

Finishing Touches: Ice with Ginger Orange Cream Cheese Icing (111) and garnish with ground cinnamon and zucchini curl.

Fall

CHUNKY MONKEY
cupcakes

Makes
24
cupcakes

Inspired by the infamous Ben and Jerry's ice creams this combination of chocolate, banana, and crunchy nuts will have you licking your wrapper clean!

WET INGREDIENTS

½ cup unsalted butter, softened

½ cup sour cream

¼ cup buttermilk

¼ cup unsweetened applesauce

½ cup vegetable oil

4 large eggs

1 Tbsp. pure vanilla

4 ripe bananas, peeled and mashed

DRY INGREDIENTS

1¼ cups brown sugar

2½ cups flour

1¼ Tbsp. baking powder

½ tsp. salt

1 tsp. ground cinnamon

1 cup chocolate chips

1. Preheat the oven to 350 degrees.

2. Beat butter and sugar at medium speed in the bowl of a stand mixer with the paddle attachment until smooth. Stop mixer and scrape down the sides of the bowl. Add sour cream, buttermilk, applesauce, oil, eggs, vanilla, and mashed bananas. Mix until ingredients are well blended and smooth.

3. In a separate bowl, sift flour, baking powder, salt, and cinnamon.

4. Turn the stand mixer onto low and add dry ingredients until just incorporated. The batter should be smooth. Stir in chocolate chips.

5. Line two standard muffin tins with paper cupcake liners. Fill each cup ⅔ full with batter. I like to use an ice cream scoop for perfect measuring every time! Bake until tops spring back to the touch of your finger, and edges are just golden brown, 20–25 minutes.

6. Remove from tins and cool completely before filling or icing.

Finishing Touches: Ice with Chocolate Buttercream (111) and drizzle with Dark Chocolate Ganache (125) and garnish with nuts.

BUTTERBEER
cupcakes

Makes
24
cupcakes

After tasting Butterbeer at Harry Potter World in Universal Studios, I decided that a cupcake needed to be made to capture the rich butterscotch flavor found in the drink. Warm butterscotch ganache makes this cupcake spell binding, and they will magically disappear.

WET INGREDIENTS

½ cup unsalted butter, softened
½ cup sour cream
½ cup cream soda
¼ cup unsweetened applesauce
3 large eggs
2 Tbsp. pure vanilla
1 Tbsp. butter extract

DRY INGREDIENTS

½ cup sugar
½ cup brown sugar
2 cups flour
1¼ Tbsp. baking powder
½ tsp. salt

1. Preheat the oven to 350 degrees.

2. Beat butter and both sugars at medium speed in the bowl of a stand mixer with the paddle attachment until smooth. Stop mixer and scrape down the sides of the bowl. Add sour cream, cream soda, applesauce, eggs, vanilla, and butter extract. Mix until ingredients are well blended and smooth.

3. In a separate bowl, sift the flour, baking powder, and salt.

4. Turn the stand mixer onto low and add the dry ingredients until just incorporated. The batter should be smooth.

5. Line two standard muffin tins with paper cupcake liners. Fill each cup ⅔ full with batter. I like to use an ice cream scoop for perfect measuring every time! Bake until tops spring back to the touch of your finger, and edges are just golden brown, 20–25 minutes.

6. Remove from tins and cool completely before filling or icing.

Finishing Touches: Ice with Butterscotch Buttercream (117) and drizzle with Butterscotch Ganache (125).

Brown

PEACH COBBLER
cupcakes

Makes

24

cupcakes

Homemade canned peaches is one of my most favorite desserts, the only thing that could make it better is putting them in a cupcake! Served with a scoop of vanilla bean ice cream, this cupcake is unbeatable.

WET INGREDIENTS

¼ cup unsalted butter, softened

½ cup sour cream

¼ cup buttermilk

¼ cup unsweetened applesauce

½ cup vegetable oil

3 large eggs

2 Tbsp. pure vanilla

1 Tbsp. vanilla bean paste

1 large fresh peach, chopped

DRY INGREDIENTS

1 cup sugar

2 cups flour

2 Tbsp. brown sugar

¼ tsp. nutmeg

¼ tsp. cinnamon

1¼ Tbsp. baking powder

½ tsp. salt

1. Preheat the oven to 350 degrees.

2. Beat butter and sugar at medium speed in the bowl of a stand mixer with the paddle attachment until smooth. Stop mixer and scrape down the sides of the bowl. Add sour cream, buttermilk, applesauce, oil, eggs, vanilla, and vanilla bean paste. Mix until ingredients are well blended and smooth.

3. In a separate bowl, sift the flour, brown sugar, spices, baking powder, and salt.

4. Turn the stand mixer onto low and add the dry ingredients until just incorporated. The batter should be smooth. Fold in chopped peaches.

5. Line two standard muffin tins with paper cupcake liners. Fill each cup ⅔ full with batter. I like to use an ice cream scoop for perfect measuring every time! Bake until tops spring back to the touch of your finger, and edges are just golden brown, 20–25 minutes.

6. Sprinkle Streusel Topping (131) over the top of each unbaked cupcake.

7. Remove from tins and cool completely before filling or icing.

Finishing Touches: Ice with Almond Honey Buttercream (117). Garnish with nutmeg and a peach slice.

Fall

APPLE SPICE
cupcakes

Makes
24
cupcakes

Apples and cinnamon make these cupcakes smell like fall. You can eat them warm with melting cinnamon cream cheese or let them cool and eat them with a hot cup of cocoa.

WET INGREDIENTS

¼ cup unsalted butter, softened

½ cup sour cream

¼ cup buttermilk

¼ cup unsweetened applesauce

½ cup vegetable oil

3 large eggs

2 Tbsp. pure vanilla

3 cups shredded gala or baking apples (about 4 medium apples)

DRY INGREDIENTS

1 cup sugar

2 cups flour

1¼ Tbsp. baking powder

1 tsp. cinnamon

1 tsp. allspice

½ tsp. salt

1. Preheat the oven to 350 degrees.

2. Beat butter and sugar at medium speed in the bowl of a stand mixer with the paddle attachment until smooth. Stop mixer and scrape down the sides of the bowl. Add sour cream, buttermilk, applesauce, oil, eggs, and vanilla. Mix until ingredients are well blended and smooth.

3. In a separate bowl, sift flour, baking powder, spices, and salt.

4. Turn the stand mixer onto low and add dry ingredients until just incorporated. The batter should be smooth. Fold in shredded apples and mix well.

5. Line two standard muffin tins with paper cupcake liners. Fill each cup ⅔ full with batter. I like to use an ice cream scoop for perfect measuring every time! Bake until tops spring back to the touch of your finger, and edges are just golden brown, 20–25 minutes.

6. Remove from tins and cool completely before filling or icing.

Finishing Touches: Ice with Brown Sugar Buttercream (119) and garnish with granola.

WHITE CHOCOLATE ORANGE CRANBERRY
cupcakes

Makes
24
cupcakes

This is truly a cupcake to be thankful for! A light citrus cupcake, sprinkled with cranberries, layered with white chocolate ganache and crowned with a swirl of orange cream cheese—who could ask for anything more?

WET INGREDIENTS

¼ cup unsalted butter, softened

½ cup sour cream

¼ cup buttermilk

¼ cup orange juice

2 Tbsp. orange zest

¼ cup unsweetened applesauce

½ cup vegetable oil

3 large eggs

2 Tbsp. pure vanilla

¾ cup fresh whole cranberries (not canned)

DRY INGREDIENTS

1 cup sugar

2 cups flour

1¼ Tbsp. baking powder

½ tsp. salt

1 cup white chocolate chips

1. Preheat the oven to 350 degrees.

2. Beat butter and sugar at medium speed in the bowl of a stand mixer with the paddle attachment until smooth. Stop mixer and scrape down the sides of the bowl. Add sour cream, buttermilk, orange juice, zest, applesauce, oil, eggs, and vanilla. Mix until ingredients are well blended and smooth.

3. In a separate bowl, sift flour, baking powder, and salt.

4. Turn the stand mixer onto low and add dry ingredients until just incorporated. The batter should be smooth. Fold in whole cranberries and white chocolate chips.

5. Line two standard muffin tins with paper cupcake liners. Fill each cup ⅔ full with batter. I like to use an ice cream scoop for perfect measuring every time! Bake until tops spring back to the touch of your finger, and edges are just golden brown, 20–25 minutes.

6. Remove from tins and cool completely before filling or icing.

Finishing Touches: Ice with White Chocolate Ganache (125) and Orange Cream Cheese Icing (110). Garnish with dried cranberries and white chocolate flakes.

Note: To keep your cranberries from sinking to the bottom of the cupcake liner, fill a bag with a small amount of flour, pour your cranberries in, and shake! Coating the berries in flour helps keep them anchored in the batter, so they do not fall to the bottom as the cupcake bakes.

Fall

APRICOT ALMOND
cupcakes

With two large apricot trees in our backyard, my mother was always looking for creative ways to use them. This inspired the creation of the Apricot Almond cupcake, which has become a favorite.

WET INGREDIENTS

¼ cup unsalted butter, softened

½ cup sour cream

¼ cup buttermilk

¼ cup unsweetened applesauce

½ cup vegetable oil

3 large eggs

2 Tbsp. pure vanilla

1 Tbsp. almond extract

½ cup finely chopped dried apricots

¼ cup slivered almonds

DRY INGREDIENTS

1 cup brown sugar

1½ cups flour

½ cup almond flour

1¼ Tbsp. baking powder

½ tsp. salt

1. Preheat the oven to 350 degrees.

2. Beat butter and sugar at medium speed in the bowl of a stand mixer with the paddle attachment until smooth. Stop mixer and scrape down the sides of the bowl. Add sour cream, buttermilk, applesauce, oil, eggs, vanilla, and almond extract. Mix until ingredients are well blended and smooth.

3. In a separate bowl, sift flour, almond flour, baking powder, and salt.

4. Turn the stand mixer onto low and add dry ingredients until just incorporated. The batter should be smooth. Fold in chopped apricots and almonds.

5. Line two standard muffin tins with paper cupcake liners. Fill each cup ⅔ full with batter. I like to use an ice cream scoop for perfect measuring every time! Bake until tops spring back to the touch of your finger, and edges are just golden brown, 20–25 minutes.

6. Remove from tins and cool completely before filling or icing.

Finishing Touches: Top with your favorite apricot preserves and almonds.

Fall

TEXAS COWBOY
cupcakes

Everything is bigger in Texas, so why not the cupcakes? This cupcake is fully loaded and is big on both texture and taste.

Makes
24
cupcakes

WET INGREDIENTS

½ cup dark chocolate chopped into small pieces

½ cup boiling water

½ cup sour cream

½ cup unsweetened applesauce

½ cup vegetable oil

3 large eggs

1 Tbsp. pure vanilla

½ cup shredded coconut

1 cup chocolate chips

½ cup chopped pecans

DRY INGREDIENTS

1 cup flour

½ cup oatmeal

½ cup sugar

½ cup brown sugar

1 Tbsp. baking powder

½ tsp. salt

½ cup Dutch-process cocoa powder

1. Preheat oven to 350 degrees.

2. Place chocolate in the bowl of a stand mixer. Pour boiling water over chocolate and let sit for 1 minute. Using the whisk attachment, mix until smooth. Scrape down the sides of the bowl. Add sour cream, applesauce, oil, eggs, and vanilla. Mix until ingredients are well blended and smooth.

3. In a separate bowl, sift flour, oatmeal, sugar, brown sugar, baking powder, salt, and cocoa.

4. Turn the stand mixer onto low, add dry ingredients, and mix until just incorporated. Batter should be smooth. Fold in coconut, chocolate chips, and pecans.

5. Line two standard muffin tins with paper cupcake liners. Fill each cup ⅔ full with batter. I like to use an ice cream scoop for perfect measuring every time! Bake until tops spring back to the touch of your finger, and a toothpick inserted into the center comes out clean, 20–25 minutes.

6. Remove from tins and cool completely before filling and icing.

Finishing Touches: Apply a single layer of Dark Chocolate Ganache (125), ice with Chocolate Buttercream (111), and garnish with caramel, coconut, or nuts.

Brown

PUMPKIN PIE
cupcakes

Makes
24
cupcakes

Although delicious anytime of the year, pumpkin cupcakes in the fall taste the best of all. Moist pumpkin cake topped with creamy whipped icing will keep you happy bite after bite!

WET INGREDIENTS

¼ cup unsalted butter, softened

½ cup sour cream

¼ cup buttermilk

¼ cup unsweetened applesauce

½ cup vegetable oil

3 large eggs

2 Tbsp. pure vanilla

1 (16-oz.) can pumpkin

DRY INGREDIENTS

½ cup sugar

½ cup plus 2 Tbsp. brown sugar

2 cups flour

1¼ Tbsp. baking powder

½ tsp. salt

2 tsp. ground cinnamon

½ tsp. ginger

⅛ tsp. nutmeg

1. Preheat the oven to 350 degrees.

2. Beat butter, white sugar, and brown sugar at medium speed in the bowl of a stand mixer with the paddle attachment until smooth. Stop mixer and scrape down the sides of the bowl. Add sour cream, buttermilk, applesauce, oil, eggs, vanilla, and canned pumpkin. Mix until ingredients are well blended and smooth.

3. In a separate bowl, sift flour, baking powder, salt, and spices.

4. Turn the stand mixer onto low and add dry ingredients until just incorporated. The batter should be smooth.

5. Line two standard muffin tins with paper cupcake liners. Fill each cup ⅔ full with batter. I like to use an ice cream scoop for perfect measuring every time! Bake until tops spring back to the touch of your finger, and edges are just golden brown, 20–25 minutes.

6. Remove from tins and cool completely before icing.

Finishing Touches: Ice with Whipped Cream Cheese Frosting (108) and garnish with cinnamon.

Brown

Winter

WHITE CHOCOLATE PASSION FRUIT
cupcakes

Makes
24
cupcakes

Inspired by the Brazilian passion fruit, maracuja, this cupcake boasts the power to make anyone fall in love. Filled with Passion Fruit Mousse and draped in White Chocolate Buttercream, no one can resist.

WET INGREDIENTS

¼ cup unsalted butter, softened

½ cup sour cream

¼ cup buttermilk

¼ cup unsweetened applesauce

½ cup vegetable oil

3 large eggs

2 Tbsp. pure vanilla

⅓ cup Passion Fruit Purée (128)

DRY INGREDIENTS

1 cup sugar

2 cups flour

1¼ Tbsp. baking powder

½ tsp. salt

1. Preheat the oven to 350 degrees.

2. Beat butter and sugar at medium speed in the bowl of a stand mixer with the paddle attachment until smooth. Stop mixer and scrape down the sides of the bowl. Add sour cream, buttermilk, applesauce, oil, eggs, vanilla, and Passion Fruit Purée. Mix until ingredients are well blended and smooth.

3. In a separate bowl, sift flour, baking powder, and salt.

4. Turn the stand mixer onto low and add dry ingredients until just incorporated. The batter should be smooth.

5. Line two standard muffin tins with paper cupcake liners. Fill each cup ⅔ full with batter. I like to use an ice cream scoop for perfect measuring every time! Bake until tops spring back to the touch of your finger, and edges are just golden brown, 20–25 minutes.

6. Remove from tins and cool completely before filling or icing.

Finishing Touches: Fill with Passion Fruit Mousse (128), layer with White Chocolate Ganache (125) and ice with White Chocolate Buttercream (118). Garnish with passion fruit paste and white chocolate straw.

Brown

BLACK FOREST
cupcakes

The combination of chocolate cake and cherry originated in Germany, but it has become an American favorite.

Makes
24
cupcakes

WET INGREDIENTS

½ cup dark chocolate chopped into small pieces

½ cup boiling marachino cherry juice

½ cup sour cream

½ cup unsweetened applesauce

½ cup vegetable oil

3 large eggs

1 Tbsp. pure vanilla

1 (8-oz.) can cherry pie filling

DRY INGREDIENTS

1½ cups flour

1 cup sugar

1 Tbsp. baking powder

½ tsp. salt

½ cup Dutch-process cocoa powder

1. Preheat oven to 350 degrees.

2. Place chocolate in the bowl of a stand mixer. Pour boiling juice over chocolate and let sit for 1 minute. Using the whisk attachment mix until smooth. Scrape down the sides of the bowl. Add sour cream, applesauce, oil, eggs, and vanilla. Mix until ingredients are well blended and smooth.

3. In a separate bowl, sift flour, sugar, baking powder, salt, and cocoa.

4. Turn the stand mixer onto low, add dry ingredients, and mix until just incorporated. Batter should be smooth.

5. Line two standard muffin tins with paper cupcake liners. Fill each cup ⅔ full with batter. I like to use an ice cream scoop for perfect measuring every time! Bake until tops spring back to the touch of your finger, and a toothpick inserted into the center comes out clean, 20–25 minutes.

6. Remove from tins and cool completely before filling and icing.

Finishing Touches: Core center of cupcakes and fill with cherry pie filling. Ice with Maraschino Cherry Buttercream (118) and garnish with Dark Chocolate Ganache (125) and a cherry.

Brown

TIRAMISU
cupcakes

Makes
24
cupcakes

Loved by so many, this is a sophisticated cupcake soaked in an espresso syrup and iced with a whipped mascarpone icing that is cool and creamy, making each bite a piece of heaven.

WET INGREDIENTS

¼ cup unsalted butter, softened

½ cup sour cream

¼ cup buttermilk

¼ cup unsweetened applesauce

½ cup vegetable oil

3 large eggs

2 Tbsp. pure vanilla

1 Tbsp. vanilla bean paste

DRY INGREDIENTS

1 cup sugar

2 cups flour

1¼ Tbsp. baking powder

½ tsp. salt

¼ cup cocoa powder
for dusting

1. Preheat the oven to 350 degrees.

2. Beat butter and sugar at medium speed in the bowl of a stand mixer with the paddle attachment until smooth. Stop mixer and scrape down the sides of the bowl. Add sour cream, buttermilk, applesauce, oil, eggs, vanilla, and vanilla bean paste. Mix until ingredients are well blended and smooth.

3. In a separate bowl, sift flour, baking powder, and salt.

4. Turn the stand mixer onto low and add dry ingredients until just incorporated. The batter should be smooth.

5. Line two standard muffin tins with paper cupcake liners. Fill each cup ⅔ full with batter. I like to use an ice cream scoop for perfect measuring every time! Bake until tops spring back to the touch of your finger, and edges are just golden brown, 20–25 minutes.

6. Remove from tins and cool completely before filling or icing.

Finishing Touches: Poke holes in each cupcake with a fork. Soak cupcakes with Espresso Syrup (131) with 1–2 tablespoons on each cupcake. Ice with Whipped Mascarpone Icing (121) and dust with cocoa powder.

Winter

RED HOT VELVET
cupcakes

Makes
24
cupcakes

Red velvet needed a little kick, so we added cinnamon and cayenne pepper to make this cupcake rock. The cinnamon cream cheese gives your taste buds a break until they're ready for the next bite!

WET INGREDIENTS

½ cup dark chocolate, chopped into small pieces

½ cup boiling water

½ cup sour cream

½ cup unsweetened applesauce

½ cup vegetable oil

3 large eggs

1 Tbsp. pure vanilla

½–1 oz. red food coloring

DRY INGREDIENTS

1½ cups flour

1 cup sugar

1 Tbsp. baking powder

½ tsp. salt

½ cup Dutch-process cocoa powder

½ tsp. cinnamon

1 tsp. cayenne powder

1. Preheat oven to 350 degrees.

2. Place chocolate in the bowl of a stand mixer. Pour boiling water over chocolate and let sit for 1 minute. Using the whisk attachment mix until smooth. Scrape down the sides of the bowl. Add sour cream, applesauce, oil, eggs, and vanilla. Mix until ingredients are well blended and smooth.

3. In a separate bowl, sift dry ingredients together.

4. Turn the stand mixer onto low, add dry ingredients, and mix until just incorporated. Batter should be smooth. Add red food coloring and mix on high speed until batter is dark red.

5. Line two standard muffin tins with paper cupcake liners. Fill each cup ⅔ full with batter. I like to use an ice cream scoop for perfect measuring every time! Bake until tops spring back to the touch of your finger, and a toothpick inserted into the center comes out clean, 22–25 minutes.

6. Remove from tins and cool completely before filling and icing.

Finishing Touches: Ice with Cinnamon Cream Cheese Icing (111).

Winter

MARBLE
cupcakes

This is the perfect cupcake when chocolate and vanilla both sound good and you can't make up your mind! Marbled together in cake and icing, this cupcake will have both sides satisfied.

Makes
24
cupcakes

WET INGREDIENTS

4 Tbsp. unsalted butter, softened

¼ cup sour cream

4 Tbsp. buttermilk

4 Tbsp. unsweetened applesauce

¼ cup vegetable oil

1 large egg plus 1 egg yolk

1 Tbsp. pure vanilla

½ Tbsp. vanilla bean paste

DRY INGREDIENTS

½ cup sugar

1 cups flour

¾ Tbsp. baking powder

¼ tsp. salt

VANILLA BEAN CUPCAKE BATTER

1. Preheat the oven to 350 degrees.

2. Beat butter and sugar at medium speed in the bowl of a stand mixer with the paddle attachment until smooth. Stop mixer and scrape down the sides of the bowl. Add sour cream, buttermilk, applesauce, oil, eggs, vanilla, and vanilla bean paste. Mix until ingredients are well blended and smooth.

3. In a separate bowl, sift flour, baking powder, and salt.

4. Turn the stand mixer onto low and add dry ingredients until just incorporated. The batter should be smooth.

Brown

WET INGREDIENTS

¼ cup dark chocolate
chopped into small pieces
¼ cup boiling water
¼ cup sour cream
¼ cup unsweetened applesauce
¼ cup vegetable oil
1 large egg plus 1 egg yolk
½ Tbsp. pure vanilla

DRY INGREDIENTS

¾ cup flour
½ cup sugar
½ Tbsp. baking powder
¼ tsp. salt
¼ cup Dutch-process cocoa
powder

UNBEATABLE CHOCOLATE CUPCAKE BATTER

1. Place chocolate in the bowl of a stand mixer. Pour boiling water over chocolate and let sit for 1 minute. Using the whisk attachment, mix until smooth. Scrape down the sides of the bowl. Add sour cream, applesauce, oil, eggs, and vanilla. Mix until ingredients are well blended and smooth.

2. In a separate bowl, sift flour, sugar, baking powder, salt, and cocoa powder.

3. Turn the stand mixer onto low, add dry ingredients, and mix until just incorporated. Batter should be smooth.

4. Line two standard muffin tins with paper cupcake liners. Fill each cup one third full with chocolate batter and one third full of vanilla bean batter. Be careful not to over fill. I like to use an ice cream scoop for perfect measuring every time! Bake until tops spring back to the touch of your finger, and a toothpick inserted into the center comes out clean, 20–25 minutes.

5. Remove from tins and cool completely before filling and icing.

Finishing Touches: Fill an icing bag with half Chocolate Buttercream (111) and half Vanilla Bean Buttercream (113). Pipe a swirl of icing on top of each cupcake.

COCONUT CARAMEL
cupcakes

Makes
24
cupcakes

Even without chocolate, these stand together. A buttery coconut cupcake dipped in caramel and topped with coconut cream cheese and toasted coconut.

WET INGREDIENTS

¼ cup unsalted butter, softened

½ cup sour cream

¼ cup coconut milk

¼ cup unsweetened applesauce

½ cup vegetable oil

3 large eggs

2 Tbsp. pure vanilla

1 Tbsp. coconut extract

DRY INGREDIENTS

1 cup sugar

2 cups flour

1¼ Tbsp. baking powder

½ tsp. salt

1 cup coconut flakes or
Toasted Coconut (126)

1. Preheat the oven to 350 degrees.

2. Beat butter and sugar at medium speed in the bowl of a stand mixer with the paddle attachment until smooth. Stop mixer and scrape down the sides of the bowl. Add sour cream, coconut milk, applesauce, oil, eggs, vanilla, and coconut extract. Mix until ingredients are well blended and smooth.

3. In a separate bowl, sift flour, baking powder, and salt.

4. Turn the stand mixer onto low and add dry ingredients until just incorporated. The batter should be smooth.

5. Line two standard muffin tins with paper cupcake liners. Fill each cup ⅔ full with batter. I like to use an ice cream scoop for perfect measuring every time! Bake until tops spring back to the touch of your finger, and edges are just golden brown, 20–25 minutes.

6. Remove from tins and cool completely before filling or icing.

Finishing Touches: Dip the top of each cupcake in Caramel Sauce (132). Place cupcakes in the fridge for 10 minutes or until caramel is set. Ice with Coconut Cream Cheese Icing (110) and garnish with coconut flakes or Toasted Coconut (126) and caramel.

Brown

TOTALLY TURTLE
cupcakes

These famous chocolates create the perfect recipe for an incredible cupcake. Chocolate caramel and nuts. What's not to love?

Makes
24
cupcakes

WET INGREDIENTS

½ cup dark chocolate
chopped into small pieces

½ cup boiling water

½ cup sour cream

½ cup unsweetened applesauce

½ cup vegetable oil

3 large eggs

1 Tbsp. pure vanilla

DRY INGREDIENTS

1½ cups flour

1 cup sugar

1 Tbsp. baking powder

½ tsp. salt

½ cup Dutch-process cocoa
powder

½ cup chopped pecans

1. Preheat oven to 350 degrees.

2. Place chocolate in the bowl of a stand mixer. Pour boiling water over chocolate and let sit for 1 minute. Using the whisk attachment, mix until smooth. Scrape down the sides of the bowl. Add sour cream, applesauce, oil, eggs, and vanilla. Mix until ingredients are well blended and smooth.

3. In a separate bowl, sift flour, sugar, baking powder, salt, and cocoa.

4. Turn the stand mixer onto low, add dry ingredients, and mix until just incorporated. Batter should be smooth. Fold in pecans.

5. Line two standard muffin tins with paper cupcake liners. Fill each cup ⅔ full with batter. I like to use an ice cream scoop for perfect measuring every time! Bake until tops spring back to the touch of your finger, and a toothpick inserted into the center comes out clean, 20–25 minutes.

6. Remove from tins and cool completely before filling and icing.

Finishing Touches: Core center of cupcakes and fill with Caramel Sauce (132) and ice with Chocolate Buttercream (111). Drizzle with Caramel Sauce (132), Dark Chocolate Ganache (125), and pecans.

Brown

CHOCOLATE-DIPPED MACAROON *cupcakes*

Makes
24
cupcakes

Inspired by our English chocolate-dipped macaroons, we decided to try a cupcake version! The icing on top of the cake is dipped in chocolate, creating a crunchy shell on the outside. Delish.

WET INGREDIENTS

¼ cup unsalted butter, softened

½ cup sour cream

¼ cup coconut milk

¼ cup unsweetened applesauce

½ cup vegetable oil

3 large eggs

2 Tbsp. pure vanilla

1 Tbsp. coconut extract

1 Tbsp. almond extract

DRY INGREDIENTS

1 cup sugar

2 cups flour

1¼ Tbsp. baking powder

½ tsp. salt

1 cup coconut flakes

½ cup chopped macadamia nuts

1. Preheat the oven to 350 degrees.

2. Beat butter and sugar at medium speed in the bowl of a stand mixer with the paddle attachment until smooth. Stop mixer and scrape down the sides of the bowl. Add sour cream, coconut milk, applesauce, oil, eggs, vanilla, coconut extract, and almond extract. Mix until ingredients are well blended and smooth.

3. In a separate bowl, sift flour, baking powder, and salt.

4. Turn the stand mixer onto low and add dry ingredients until just incorporated. The batter should be smooth. Fold in coconut and macadamia nuts.

5. Line two standard muffin tins with paper cupcake liners. Fill each cup ⅔ full with batter. I like to use an ice cream scoop for perfect measuring every time! Bake until tops spring back to the touch of your finger, and edges are just golden brown, 20–25 minutes.

6. Remove from tins and cool completely before filling or icing.

Finishing Touches: Ice cupcakes with Vanilla Bean Buttercream (113). Melt 1 (16 oz.) bag of chocolate candy melts in a deep microwave-safe bowl. Flip the iced cupcake upside down and dip the icing into the melted chocolate. Quickly flip it right side up and set on a cookie sheet to cool. Garnish with coconut flakes or Toasted Coconut (126).

Winter

RASPBERRY ALMOND
cupcakes

Makes
24
cupcakes

A slight variation to our popular raspberry swirl cupcake. These will leave you asking for more!

WET INGREDIENTS

¼ cup unsalted butter, softened

½ cup sour cream

¼ cup buttermilk

¼ cup unsweetened applesauce

½ cup vegetable oil

3 large eggs

2 Tbsp. pure vanilla

1 Tbsp. almond extract

½ cup Raspberry Purée (128)

DRY INGREDIENTS

1 cup sugar

2 cups flour

1¼ Tbsp. baking powder

½ tsp. salt

1. Preheat the oven to 350 degrees.

2. Beat butter and sugar at medium speed in the bowl of a stand mixer with the paddle attachment until smooth. Stop mixer and scrape down the sides of the bowl. Add sour cream, buttermilk, applesauce, oil, eggs, vanilla, and almond extract. Mix until ingredients are well blended and smooth.

3. In a separate bowl, sift the flour, baking powder, and salt.

4. Turn the stand mixer onto low and add dry ingredients until just incorporated. The batter should be smooth. Fold in Raspberry Purée until batter is marbled.

5. Line two standard muffin tins with paper cupcake liners. Fill each cup ⅔ full with batter. I like to use an ice cream scoop for perfect measuring every time! Bake until tops spring back to the touch of your finger, and edges are just golden brown, 20–25 minutes.

6. Remove from tins and cool completely before filling or icing.

Finishing Touches: Ice with Almond Honey Buttercream (117) and garnish with a single fresh raspberry and chopped almonds.

Note: Be careful not to over mix when adding the Raspberry Purée. The batter should be marbled, not pink.

Brown

WHITE CHOCOLATE MACADAMIA NUT
cupcakes

While visiting Hawaii, I had some of the most delicious macadamia nut ice cream ever! I decided then and there that these nuts needed to find their way into a cupcake. Pairing it with white chocolate is a cookie favorite and tastes even better in a cupcake!

Makes
24
cupcakes

WET INGREDIENTS

¼ cup unsalted butter, softened

3 large eggs

½ cup sour cream

¼ cup unsweetened applesauce

½ cup vegetable oil

2 Tbsp. pure vanilla

DRY INGREDIENTS

1 cup sugar

2 cups flour

1½ cups coarsely chopped macadamia nuts

1¼ Tbsp. baking powder

½ tsp. salt

1 cup white chocolate chips

1. Preheat the oven to 350 degrees.

2. Beat butter and sugar at medium speed in the bowl of a stand mixer with the paddle attachment until smooth. Stop mixer and scrape down the sides of the bowl. Add eggs one at a time, beating well after each addition. Beat in sour cream, applesauce, oil, and vanilla. Mix until ingredients are well blended and smooth.

3. In a separate bowl, sift flour, macadamia nuts, baking powder, and salt. Slowly add to the wet ingredients and beat until smooth, about 2 minutes.

4. Fold in white chocolate chips.

5. Line two standard muffin tins with paper cupcake liners. Fill each cup ⅔ full with batter. I like to use an ice cream scoop for perfect measuring every time! Bake until tops spring back to the touch of your finger, and edges are just golden brown, 20–22 minutes.

6. Remove from tins and cool completely before filling or icing.

Finishing Touches: Ice with White Chocolate Buttercream (118) and garnish with white chocolate flakes and macadamia nuts.

Icings

WHIPPED CREAM
frosting

1 cup heavy whipping cream

1 tsp. vanilla extract

1 Tbsp. sugar

1. Beat together the heavy whipping cream, vanilla, and sugar until soft peaks form.

WHIPPED CREAM CHEESE
icing

1 pint heavy whipping cream

1 (8-oz.) pkg. cream cheese, softened

½ cup powdered sugar

1. Beat whipping cream until stiff peaks form. In a separate bowl, mix softened cream cheese and powdered sugar until smooth. Fold in the whipped cream until smooth and creamy.

LEMON WHIPPED
CREAM CHEESE *icing*

1 batch Whipped Cream Cheese Icing (108)

2 Tbsp. lemon juice

1 Tbsp. lemon zest

1. Follow directions for Whipped Cream Cheese Icing.

2. Fold in lemon juice and fresh lemon zest. Mix until smooth.

CREAM CHEESE
icing

1 (8-oz.) pkg. cream cheese, softened

4 Tbsp. butter, softened

1 tsp. vanilla

2½–3 cups powdered sugar

1. Beat cream cheese and butter together until smooth and creamy. Make sure there are no chunks! Add 2 cups of powdered sugar and beat until smooth. Add vanilla and remaining powdered sugar and beat until light and fluffy.

COCONUT CREAM CHEESE
icing

1 batch Cream Cheese Icing (108)

¼ cup coconut milk

2 tsp. coconut extract

1–2 cups powdered sugar

1. Follow directions for Cream Cheese Icing.
2. Turn mixer speed to low and add coconut milk, coconut extract and powdered sugar, beating until smooth and creamy.

ORANGE CREAM CHEESE
icing

1 batch Cream Cheese Icing (108)

2 Tbsp. fresh orange juice

1 Tbsp. orange zest

1. Follow directions for Cream Cheese Icing.
2. Fold in fresh orange juice and orange zest.

HONEY CREAM CHEESE
icing

1 batch Cream Cheese Icing (108)

4 Tbsp. honey

1. Follow directions for Cream Cheese Icing.
2. Turn mixer speed to low and add honey. Beat until smooth and creamy.

CREAM CHEESE HONEY
glaze

1 batch Cream Cheese Icing (108)

4 Tbsp. honey

1 Tbsp. cinnamon

¼ cup milk

1. Follow directions for Cream Cheese Icing.
2. Turn mixer speed to low and add honey, cinnamon, and milk. Beat until smooth and creamy.

PINK LEMON CREAM CHEESE
icing

1 batch Cream Cheese Icing (108)

3 Tbsp. lemon juice

1 Tbsp. lemon zest

2–3 drops pink food coloring

1–2 cups powdered sugar

1. Follow directions for Cream Cheese Icing.
2. Turn mixer speed to low and add lemon juice, lemon zest, pink food coloring, and powdered sugar. Beat until smooth and creamy.

GINGER ORANGE CREAM CHEESE *icing*

1 batch Cream Cheese Icing (108)
1 Tbsp. orange juice
2 tsp. orange zest
1 tsp. ground ginger
1 tsp. ground cinnamon
1–2 cups powdered sugar

1. Follow directions for Cream Cheese Icing.
2. Turn mixer speed to low and add orange juice, orange zest, ginger, cinnamon, and powdered sugar. Beat until smooth and creamy.

CINNAMON CREAM CHEESE *icing*

1 batch Cream Cheese Icing (108)
½ Tbsp. cinnamon

1. Follow directions for Cream Cheese Icing.
2. Turn mixer speed to low and add cinnamon. Beat until smooth and creamy.

CHOCOLATE *buttercream*

1 lb. butter, softened
2 lbs. plus 1½ cups powdered sugar
½ cup cocoa powder
4–6 Tbsp. milk
1½ Tbsp. vanilla
¼ cup Dark Chocolate Ganache (125)
pinch of salt

1. In a stand mixer bowl with the paddle attachment, beat butter until light, completely smooth, and fluffy.
2. Turn the mixer speed to low and add half of the powdered sugar. Add cocoa powder. Mix until smooth.
3. Alternately add remaining powdered sugar and milk until smooth and creamy. Add vanilla, ganache, and salt. Beat until smooth.

VANILLA BEAN
buttercream

1 lb. butter, softened
2 lbs. plus 1½ cups powdered sugar
4 Tbsp. milk
1½ Tbsp. vanilla
1 Tbsp. vanilla bean paste
pinch of salt

1. In a stand mixer bowl with the paddle attachment, beat butter until light, completely smooth, and fluffy.
2. Turn the mixer speed to low and add half of the powdered sugar. Mix until smooth. Alternately add remaining powdered sugar and milk until smooth and creamy.
3. Add vanilla, vanilla bean paste, and salt. Beat until smooth.

STRAWBERRY
buttercream

1 lb. butter, softened
2 lbs. plus 1½ cups powdered sugar
4 Tbsp. milk
1½ Tbsp. vanilla
pinch of salt
½ cup Strawberry Purée (128)

1. In a stand mixer bowl with the paddle attachment, beat butter until light, completely smooth, and fluffy.
2. Turn the mixer speed to low and add half of the powdered sugar. Mix until smooth.
3. Alternately add remaining powder sugar and milk until smooth and creamy.
4. Add vanilla, salt, and Strawberry Purée. Beat until smooth.

TANGERINE
buttercream

1 cup butter, softened
3 cups powdered sugar
1 tsp. vanilla
1–2 Tbsp. tangerine juice
1 Tbsp. tangerine zest

1. Beat butter until smooth and creamy. Add 1½ cups of powdered sugar. Beat until smooth.
2. Add vanilla, tangerine juice, and zest.
3. Add remaining powdered sugar and beat until light and fluffy.

Icings

BLACKBERRY
buttercream

1 lb. butter, softened

2 lbs. plus 1½ cups powdered sugar

4 Tbsp. milk

1½ Tbsp. vanilla

pinch of salt

½ cup Blackberry Purée (128)

1. In a stand mixer bowl with the paddle attachment, beat butter until light, completely smooth, and fluffy.

2. Turn the mixer speed to low and add half of the powdered sugar. Mix until smooth.

3. Alternately add remaining powder sugar and milk until smooth and creamy. Add vanilla and salt, and Blackberry Purée. Beat until smooth.

MANGO
buttercream

1 lb. butter, softened

2 lbs. plus 1½ cups powdered sugar

4 Tbsp. milk

1½ Tbsp. vanilla

pinch of salt

¼ cup canned (or fresh) mango, puréed

1. In a stand mixer bowl with the paddle attachment, beat butter until light, completely smooth, and fluffy.

2. Turn the mixer speed to low and add half of the powdered sugar. Mix until smooth.

3. Alternately add remaining powdered sugar and milk until smooth and creamy.

4. Add vanilla and salt. Add puréed mango. Beat until smooth.

5. Add ½ cup more powdered sugar if needed.

WATERMELON
buttercream

1 lb. butter, softened
2 lbs. plus 1½ cups powdered sugar
2 Tbsp. milk
1½ Tbsp. watermelon extract or
1½ tsp. watermelon oil
2 Tbsp. lime juice
pinch of salt
2–3 drops pink food coloring

1. In a stand mixer bowl with the paddle attachment, beat butter until light, completely smooth, and fluffy.

2. Turn the mixer speed to low and add half of the powdered sugar. Mix until smooth.

3. Alternately add remaining powdered sugar and milk until smooth and creamy.

4. Add watermelon extract, lime juice, salt, and food coloring. Beat until smooth.

GRENADINE
buttercream

1½ lbs. butter, softened
2 lbs. powdered sugar
2 Tbsp. milk
4–6 Tbsp. grenadine syrup
pinch of salt

1. In a stand mixer bowl with the paddle attachment, beat butter until light, completely smooth, and fluffy.

2. Turn the mixer speed to low and add half of the powdered sugar. Mix until smooth.

3. Alternately add remaining powdered sugar and milk until smooth and creamy.

4. Add grenadine syrup and salt. Beat until smooth.

BUTTERSCOTCH
buttercream

1 lb. butter, softened
2 lbs. plus 1½ cups powdered sugar
4 Tbsp. milk
1 Tbsp. vanilla
½ cup Butterscotch Ganache (125)
pinch of salt

1. In a stand mixer bowl with the paddle attachment, beat butter until light, completely smooth, and fluffy.
2. Turn the mixer speed to low and add half of the powdered sugar. Mix until smooth.
3. Alternately add remaining powdered sugar and milk until smooth and creamy.
4. Add vanilla, butterscotch ganache, and salt. Beat until smooth.

ALMOND HONEY
buttercream

1 lb. butter, softened
2 lbs. plus 1½ cups powdered sugar
4 Tbsp. milk
1 Tbsp. vanilla
1 Tbsp. almond extract
4 Tbsp. honey
pinch of salt

1. In a stand mixer bowl with the paddle attachment, beat butter until light, completely smooth, and fluffy.
2. Turn the mixer speed to low and add half of the powdered sugar. Mix until smooth.
3. Alternately add remaining powdered sugar and milk until smooth and creamy.
4. Add vanilla, almond extract, honey, and salt. Beat until smooth.

MARASCHINO CHERRY
buttercream

1 lb. butter, softened
2 lbs. plus 1½ cups powdered sugar
2 Tbsp. milk
1½ Tbsp. vanilla
¼ cup marachino cherry juice
pinch of salt

1. In a stand mixer bowl with the paddle attachment, beat butter until light, completely smooth, and fluffy.
2. Turn the mixer speed to low and add half of the powdered sugar. Mix until smooth.
3. Alternately add remaining powdered sugar and milk until smooth and creamy.
4. Add vanilla, marachino juice, and salt. Beat until smooth.

WHITE CHOCOLATE
buttercream

1 lb. butter, softened
2 lbs. plus 1½ cups powdered sugar
4 Tbsp. milk
1½ Tbsp. vanilla
1 Tbsp. vanilla bean paste
pinch of salt
2 cups cold White Chocolate Ganache (125)

1. In a stand mixer bowl with the paddle attachment, beat butter until light, completely smooth, and fluffy.
2. Turn the mixer speed to low and add half of the powdered sugar. Mix until smooth. Alternately add remaining powdered sugar and milk until smooth and creamy.
3. Add vanilla, vanilla bean paste, and salt. Beat until smooth.
4. Fold 2 cups cool white chocolate ganache into buttercream and beat until smooth.

BROWN SUGAR
buttercream

1 cup dark brown sugar

½ cup water

3 large egg whites

½ tsp. salt

½ tsp. lemon juice

1½ cups butter, softened

2 tsp. vanilla

1. Stir together brown sugar and water in a small saucepan. Bring to boil over high heat, washing down the sides of the pan with a pastry brush dipped in water to prevent crystallization.

2. When the sugar reaches a boil, begin beating the egg whites and salt in the bowl of a stand mixer with the whisk attachment on high speed until frothy. Add the lemon juice and beat on medium speed until soft peaks begin to form. Check the temperature of the cooking sugar by using a candy thermometer.

3. When the syrup reaches 238–240°F, remove the pan from the heat and pour the sugar into a glass measuring cup. Slowly pour the mixture down the side and into the bowl of the egg whites while it is mixing at high speed. Beat the meringue until it is cool to the touch. Scrape the sides of the bowl to make sure the ingredients are mixed together well, about 5 minutes.

4. With the mixer on medium speed, gradually add the butter in small chunks. Continue beating until the mixture is smooth. Add the vanilla and beat for another minute. The icing will separate for a time and look curdled, but will come back together as the ingredients emulsify.

CHOCOLATE MALT
buttercream

1½ cups finely chopped milk chocolate

1 cup malted milk powder

1 cup heavy cream

1 stick butter, softened

1. Place the chopped chocolate in the bowl of a stand mixer.

2. In a small saucepan stir together the malted milk powder and heavy cream. Heat over medium heat, stirring constantly until mixture comes to a simmer.

3. Pour the cream mixture over the chocolate and let sit for one minute. Whisk together until smooth and creamy. Cover with plastic wrap and refrigerate until chilled, about 2 hours.

4. When the chocolate mixture is chilled, cut the butter into cubes and start mixing on low. Add cubes one at a time until completely incorporated. Increase to medium speed and beat until the frosting is smooth and thick.

RASPBERRY LIME CREAM *icing*

1 cup plus 1 Tbsp. powdered sugar
1 (8-oz.) pkg. cream cheese
½ cup cold Raspberry Lime Curd (127)
1½ cups heavy cream
1 tsp. lime zest

1. In a small bowl, whisk together powdered sugar, cream cheese, and Raspberry Lime Curd.

2. In another bowl, using a stand mixture and the whisk attachment, beat cream on high until stiff peaks form.

3. Fold the two mixtures and lime zest together until smooth.

DULCE DE LECHE *icing*

½ cup butter, softened
1 (8-oz.) cream cheese, softened
¾ cup store-bought dulce de leche
3 cups powdered sugar
1 tsp. vanilla
¼ tsp. salt

1. In a stand mixer bowl with the paddle attachment, beat butter and cream cheese until completely smooth, about 10 minutes.

2. Turn mixer speed to low and add dulce de leche and powdered sugar. Beat until smooth.

3. Add vanilla and salt, and beat until light and creamy.

WHIPPED MASCARPONE
icing

1 (8-oz.) pkg. mascarpone cheese
1 cup powdered sugar
pinch of salt
1 tsp. vanilla
1½ cups heavy cream

1. In one bowl, combine mascarpone cheese, powdered sugar, salt, and vanilla. Stir together until smooth and set aside.

2. Pour whipping cream into a separate bowl. Using an electric mixture, beat until stiff peaks form. Do not overmix. Fold whipped cream into the mascarpone mixture until combined. Use immediately.

CHERRY COKE
glaze

3 Tbsp. Cherry Coke
1 cup powdered sugar

1. Pour cherry coke into a medium sized bowl. Slowly add 1 cup powdered sugar and mix with a wire whisk until smooth.

2. Spoon a small amount onto tops of cupcakes.

Fillings & Toppings

WHITE CHOCOLATE
ganache

2 cups good quality white
chocolate, finely chopped

¾ cups heavy cream

1. Place chocolate in a large heatproof bowl. Bring cream to a simmer on stovetop until just before boiling, then pour mixture over chocolate. Let stand, without stirring, until the chocolate begins to melt.

2. Using a whisk, start at the center of the mixture and stir until the chocolate and cream are combined and smooth. Do not overmix.

3. Place a layer of plastic wrap directly on the ganache and refrigerate, stirring every 5 minutes until the mixture begins to cool and thicken.

DARK CHOCOLATE
ganache

2 cups good quality bittersweet
chocolate, finely chopped

1 cup heavy cream

1. Place chocolate in a large heatproof bowl. Bring cream to a simmer on stovetop until just before boiling, then pour mixture over chocolate. Let stand, without stirring, until the chocolate begins to melt.

2. Using a whisk, start at the center of the mixture and stir until the chocolate and cream are combined and smooth. Do not overmix.

3. Place a layer of plastic wrap directly on the ganache and refrigerate, stirring every 5 minutes until the mixture begins to cool and thicken.

BUTTERSCOTCH
ganache

1 pkg. high quality butterscotch chips

1 cup heavy cream

1. Heat cream and pour over chips. Whisk until smooth.

Note: Mixture will be thinner than normal ganache.

Fillings & Toppings

TOASTED COCONUT

1. Preheat oven to 350 degrees. Spread coconut evenly on baking sheet lined with parchment paper. Toast coconut, stirring occasionally, until it begins to brown, about 8–10 minutes. Cool completely before using.

TOASTED COCONUT CREAM *filling*

1 cup sweetened flake coconut

4 egg yolks

½ cup sugar

⅛ teaspoon salt

1 stick butter, room temperature

¼ cup coconut milk

¾ cup whole milk

1 tsp. vanilla extract

1. Follow directions for Toasted Coconut.

2. Whisk the egg yolks, sugar, and salt together in a heavy-bottomed saucepan. Then whisk in the butter, coconut milk, milk, and vanilla. Cook over medium-low heat, stirring continuously until thickened, about 10 minutes. The pastry cream will have a pudding-like consistency. Transfer it to a clean metal bowl set over an ice bath.

3. When the pastry cream has cooled, stir in the toasted coconut. Cover the surface directly with plastic wrap, and refrigerate until chilled, at least 3 hours.

Yield: 1½ cups

LIME *curd*

¾ cup egg yolks

¾ cup whole eggs

¾ cup sugar

¾ cup fresh lime juice

zest of 4 limes

¾ cup butter, softened

1. Mix the egg yolks, eggs, sugar, and lime juice together.

2. Add the lime zest and butter.

3. Cook over a water bath until thickened. Check the temperature with a candy thermometer, making sure it reaches 160 degrees.

4. Strain and mix with a whisk until smooth. Refrigerate until needed. Mixture should be completely cool before using.

Note: Do not skip the straining process! This will catch the unwanted zest and overcooked eggs, resulting in a smooth and tangy lime curd.

RASPBERRY LIME
curd

1 cup frozen raspberries
¾ cup egg yolks
¾ cup whole eggs
¾ cup sugar
¾ cup fresh lime juice
¾ cup butter, softened
zest of 4 limes

1. Press raspberries through a fine sieve to extract all the pulp. Set aside.

2. Mix the egg yolks, eggs, sugar, and lemon juice together.

3. Add the lemon zest, butter, and raspberry pulp.

4. Cook over a water bath until thickened. Check the temperature with a candy thermometer, making sure it reaches 160 degrees.

5. Strain and mix with a whisk until smooth. Refrigerate until needed. Mixture should be completely cool before using.

Note: Do not skip the straining process! This will catch the unwanted zest and overcooked eggs, resulting in a smooth and tangy lime curd.

LEMON
cream

¾ cup egg yolks
¾ cup whole eggs
¾ cup sugar
¾ cup fresh lemon juice
zest of 4 lemons
¾ cup butter, softened

1. Mix the egg yolks, eggs, sugar, and lemon juice together.

2. Add the lemon zest and butter.

3. Cook over a water bath until thickened. Check the temperature with a candy thermometer, making sure it reaches 160 degrees.

4. Strain and mix with a whisk until smooth. Refrigerate until needed. Mixture should be completely cool before using.

Note: Do not skip the straining process! This will catch the unwanted zest and overcooked eggs, resulting in a smooth and tangy lemon curd.

CREAM
filling

1 (8-oz.) pkg. cream cheese

1 cup powdered sugar

Pinch of salt

1 tsp. vanilla

1½ cups heavy cream

1. Combine cream cheese, powdered sugar, salt, and vanilla. Stir together until smooth and set aside.

2. Pour whipping cream into the bowl of an electric mixer and beat until stiff peaks form. Do not overmix.

3. Fold whipped cream into the cream cheese mixture until combined. Use immediately.

BERRY
purée (Raspberry, Strawberry, or Blackberry)

1½ cups fresh or frozen berries

¼ cup sugar

2 Tbsp. lemon juice

1. Combine berries, sugar, and lemon juice in a sauce pan and cook over medium heat, stirring occasionally until a liquid forms.

2. Continue cooking until the mixture starts to thicken.

3. Pour sauce into a fine sieve set over a bowl. Use a rubber spatula to stir and press the purée through the sieve; throw the seeds away.

4. Taste and refrigerate. May be frozen for up to 1 month.

Yield: Approximately 1 cup of purée.

PASSION FRUIT
purée

8–10 passion fruits

1. Break passion fruits in half, and scoop fruit out into a bowl. Mix with your hands to soften the pulp. Strain the pulp through a sieve.

PASSION FRUIT
mousse

1 cup heavy cream

2 Tbsp. sugar

½ cup Passion Fruit Purée (128)

½ can sweetened condensed milk

1. Whisk cream until soft peaks begin to form. Do not overmix. Add powdered sugar and whisk until combined. Add purée and condensed milk. Use immediately.

EGG-LESS CHOCOLATE CHIP COOKIE DOUGH

1 stick unsalted butter, softened
½ cup brown sugar
¼ cup sugar
½ tsp. pure vanilla
½ tsp. salt
2 Tbsp. milk
1 cup flour
¾ cup chocolate chips

1. Beat butter and sugar at medium speed in the bowl of a stand mixer with the paddle attachment until smooth. Stop mixer and scrape down the sides of the bowl.
2. Add vanilla and salt. Mixture will be crumbly.
3. Add milk and flour. Mix until a dough forms.
4. Fold in chocolate chips.

STRAWBERRY
filling

½ cup fresh chopped strawberries
¼ cup Strawberry Purée (128)

1. Fold together until mixed. Core center of cupcakes and fill with strawberry filling using a spoon.

STREUSEL
topping

1 cup flour
1 cup oatmeal
1 cup brown sugar
2¼ tsp. ground cinnamon
¼ tsp. salt
1½ sticks unsalted butter, softened

1. Mix together the flour, oatmeal, brown sugar, cinnamon, and salt. Cut in the butter with your fingers until combined, but still crumbly.

ESPRESSO
syrup

⅓ cup sugar
2 Tbsp. espresso powder
1 Tbsp. coffee extract

1. In a small saucepan, combine the water, sugar, and espresso powder.
2. Heat over medium-high heat until the sugar is dissolved and liquid is boiling, stirring occasionally. Once boiling, quickly remove from heat and stir in the coffee extract.
3. When liquid is cool, poke holes into cupcakes with a fork and soak the cupcake with the espresso syrup by pouring 1–2 tablespoons over each cupcake.

CARAMEL
sauce

½ cup butter
1 cup brown sugar
½ cup heavy cream

1. In a small saucepan, melt butter and stir in brown sugar and cream.

2. Bring to a boil, over medium to high heat for about 5 minutes. Reduce heat and simmer for 3–4 minutes or until caramel sauce begins to thicken.

3. Remove from heat stirring occasionally until cool and ready to use.

THREE-MILK
recipe

½ cup evaporated milk
½ cup sweetened condensed milk
½ cup whole milk

1. Pour all three milks into one bowl and stir together.

2. Poke holes into cupcakes using a fork, and pour a small amount of the milk mixture over each cupcake until soaked.

COOKING MEASUREMENT EQUIVALENTS

Cups	Tablespoons	Fluid Ounces
⅛ cup	2 Tbsp.	1 fl. oz.
¼ cup	4 Tbsp.	2 fl. oz.
⅓ cup	5 Tbsp. + 1 tsp.	
½ cup	8 Tbsp.	4 fl. oz.
⅔ cup	10 Tbsp. + 2 tsp.	
¾ cup	12 Tbsp.	6 fl. oz.
1 cup	16 Tbsp.	8 fl. oz.

Cups	Fluid Ounces	Pints/Quarts/Gallons
1 cup	8 fl. oz.	½ pint
2 cups	16 fl. oz.	1 pint = ½ quart
3 cups	24 fl. oz.	1½ pints
4 cups	32 fl. oz.	2 pints = 1 quart
8 cups	64 fl. oz.	2 quarts = ½ gallon
16 cups	128 fl. oz.	4 quarts = 1 gallon

Other Helpful Equivalents

1 Tbsp.	3 tsp.
8 oz.	½ lb.
16 oz.	1 lb.

METRIC MEASUREMENT EQUIVALENTS

Approximate Weight Equivalents

Ounces	Pounds	Grams
4 oz.	¼ lb.	113 g
5 oz.		142 g
6 oz.		170 g
8 oz.	½ lb.	227 g
9 oz.		255 g
12 oz.	¾ lb.	340 g
16 oz.	1 lb.	454 g

Approximate Volume Equivalents

Cups	US Fluid Ounces	Milliliters
⅛ cup	1 fl. oz.	30 ml
¼ cup	2 fl. oz.	59 ml
½ cup	4 fl. oz.	118 ml
¾ cup	6 fl. oz.	177 ml
1 cup	8 fl. oz.	237 ml

Other Helpful Equivalents

½ tsp.	2½ ml
1 tsp.	5 ml
1 Tbsp.	15 ml

INDEX

Index

ABOUT THE AUTHOR

Janell Brown joined the cupcake industry when, faced with financial struggles, she decided to take her hobby to the next level. In her adventure, she has turned a fun stay-at-home-mom craft into a successful business. Her story is one of hard work, determination, challenges, and success. In 2012, she won *Cupcake Wars* on Food Network, which launched her business to new levels. Janell resides in West Jordan, Utah, with her husband and four children. You can see more of her work at www.OneSweetSlice.com.

ABOUT THE PHOTOGRAPHER

Jen Korth, owner of Jen Korth Photography, is an avid photographer in Northern Utah, whose business has taken her to all corners of the world. She has photographed in China and many European countries, her favorite being Paris. Specializing in family portraiture, Jen has also branched out into food photography. You can see more of her work in Janell's first cupcake book, *One Sweet Cupcake.* She is currently studying graphic design and hopes to make it her new business venture soon.

Jen has a wonderful husband and four children, and all keep her on her toes daily. She loves creating, crafting, and dreaming up future plans and travels. Jen is inspired by all things beautiful, delightful, and healthy, with a sweet cupcake or two on the side, of course.

Her work can be seen on her website www.JenKorthPhotography.com and she can be reach at JenKorth@hotmail.com.

ACKNOWLEDGMENTS & THANKS

First, I have to give thanks to my Father in Heaven for sticking with me, my husband, Trent, and our crazy family through the past few years. We are on an exciting, discouraging, unpredictable, uplifting, eye-opening, life-changing, and unforgettable ride. He has stuck with us, never failing. To Trent, for being my realist, confidant, comforter, strength, best friend, and for the unconditional love you give to me. I wouldn't want to be on this ride with anyone else. Let's be honest, I probably would have jumped off by now if it wasn't for you. To our amazing children, who now know how to say the word *fondant* properly, have become so responsible, love to eat what they create, and talk about who and how they are going to run the cake shop one day—I LOVE YOU! I hope that I can remember to be as forgiving, kind, loving, and honest as you all are. You are without guile and pure in heart, a perfect example for any business owner. Thank you to our parents, brothers, and sisters! Your listening, support, babysitting, and advice have meant the world to us. We cannot do this with out you! Thank you to our friends and neighbors who keep coming in to buy cupcakes, and who are so understanding and supportive of our busy lives. I wish I could list you all! Thank you, Jen, for being willing to tackle this project a second time, and for the beautiful pictures you take. Thank you to Cedar Fort for giving me the opportunity to put these delicious recipes together, and for pushing me to get it finished. And finally, thank you to the wonderful team at One Sweet Slice. You truly make it all happen!

144